FAQ – BRAND MANAGEMENT

HIMANSHU VAIDYA

How difficult it is to be simple
Vincent van Gogh

Preface

This book is the second book in the FAQ series. The first was 'FAQ-Psychoanalysis'. The FAQ series is anchored on the theme, 'Knowledge is delicious, don't fear learning'. Endeavor is to make knowledge simple and delicious and provide an inviting entry into a subject after which the reader can explore deeper.

'FAQ–Brand Management', provides a simple exposition of area of Brand management. It covers the area from its history to contemporary concepts and the context. The coverage is comprehensive and original and I hope readers will find it rewarding.

Brand management is an area that rightfully needs audio-visual material and case studies for developing a complete feel of the area and competence therein. In the next edition of this book an enclosed CD should complete the book even more. I would invite readers to write to me their opinions and expectations that remain unaddressed by this edition.

Hopefully the FAQ series will stand out as a structure and a genre that will develop further making knowledge more democratic. Naturally a 'video FAQ' is the natural next step to take for all books in the FAQ series. The next book being planned in this series is 'FAQ-Hinduism'. Hope my belief in 'FAQ' stands true.

Life and Death of Brands

Brands have no right to exist. They are not guaranteed by the constitution. There is no economic law that expects them to fuel supply or demand. They carry no inbred immune system. It is possible to sell a product or service without creating an elaborate brand; in fact, it happens all the time. It would take some major adjustments, but global economies would eventually survive if brands were to fall out of sight and never be heard from again. While brands admittedly have become the foundation of our commercial markets, they are, hard as it might to be to accept, dispensable.

Lynn B Upshaw

A Product is something that is made in a factory, a Brand is something that is bought by a customer. A product can be copied by a competitor, a Brand is unique. A product can be quickly outdated; a successful Brand is timeless

Stephen King
WPP Group, London

INDEX

2 BRAND MANAGEMENT: FUNDAMENTAL CONCEPTS

a) **CONSUMER'S BRAND ADOPTION PROCESS**

1. BRAND AWARENESS
2. BRAND COMPREHENSION
3. BRAND PREFERENCE
4. BRAND USAGE
5. BRAND LOYALTY

b) **SEGMENTATION – TARGETTING – POSITIONING (S-T-P)**

c) **BRAND EXPERIENCE**

d) **BRAND IMAGE**

e) **BRAND PERSONALITY**

f) **BRAND IDENTITY**

g) **BRAND ESSENCE**

PART V

CONTEMPORARY ISSUES IN BRAND MANAGEMENT

14 CONTEMPORARY ISSUES IN BRAND MANAGEMENT

a) **EMPLOYER BRANDING**

b) CO-BRANDING

c) **PR LED BRAND MANAGEMENT**

d) BRAND COMMODITISATION

e) **CAUSE LED BRAND MANAGEMENT**

f) EXPERIENTIAL BRAND MANAGEMENT

g) **BRAND MANAGEMENT IN A DIGITAL ERA**

h) EMPTY BRANDS

ANNEXURE

a) GOOD RESOURCES ON BRAND MANAGEMENT
- BOOKS
- WEB SITES
- VIDEOS

PART I

BRAND: MEANING, SCOPE, FUNDAMENTAL CONCEPTS

"Brand" had been with us since human time began. Millennia before marketing coined the term "branding," the how, when, and why of people "attaching" to a person, product, or idea, has been nothing less than the engine of history.

Bob Deutsch, president, Brain Sells

Looking at the economic importance of brands on an international stage, the 100 most valuable brands in 2008 were worth over $1.2 trillion, which would make them the 11th biggest 'country 'in the world by GDP, ahead of India and just behind Brazil.

Rita Clifton, Chairman, InterBrand

BRAND: MEANING AND SCOPE

If you are not a brand, you are a commodity

Philip Kotler

1) **What is a Brand?**

   A product can be purchased either as a Commodity or as a Brand. When you buy Salt from a hawker who sells Salt without associating any name with it (it is more prevalent in under developed economies) then you are purchasing the product as a Commodity. However if you purchase Salt branded under some name viz. Tata Salt or Captain Cook then you are buying the product as a Brand.

   When the economy is under developed most products are sold as commodities. As the economy develops more products are sold as brands. 'Brand commerce' thus succeeds and exceeds 'Commodity commerce' as the economy develops.

Brand is a name and/or a symbol (logo) which is used to sell a product. Some brands are only names like Versace while some like General Motors have both a name and a symbol (logo).

Brand helps the customer trace the origin of the product to its producer and thus reward or punish the producer based on the level of customer satisfaction derived in consumption of the product.

Branding as an action is defined by Oxford Dictionary as, 'to mark indelibly as proof of ownership, as a sign of quality, or for any other purpose'

2) **How do you define a Brand?**

'Brand' as a term has been variedly defined by varied experts, some of the popular definitions are given here,

The American Marketing Association defines a Brand as "A name, term, design, symbol, or any other feature that identifies one seller's good or service as distinct from those of other sellers. The legal term for Brand is a 'trademark'. A Brand may identify one item, a family of items, or all items of that seller."

American Marketing Association

A Brand is a name, term, sign symbol or design or a combination of them, intended to identify the goods or services of one seller or a group of sellers and to differentiate them from those of competitors

Philip Kotler

A successful Brand is an identifiable product, service, place or person, augmented in such a way that the buyer or user perceives relevant, unique added values which match their needs most closely. Furthermore, its success results from being able to sustain these added values in face of competition

Leslie & Malcolm, Creating Powerful Brands

A Brand is a distinguishing name and/or symbol (such as a logo, trade mark, or package design) intended to identify the goods or services of either one seller or a group of sellers, and to differentiate those goods or services from those of competitors

David Aaker

3) What has been the 'history of the Brand' in human civilization?

'Branding' has been used in human civilization since ancient times. It started with 'branding cattle' to establish its ownership. The branding of farm animals in Egypt in 2700 BC to avoid theft may be considered the earliest form of branding. 'Branding' in a literal sense was then used to 'Brand' criminals where a mark was put on their body. Property in terms of equipment, residences and even women were Branded. In the slave era, the slaves were 'branded' with the mark of their owners. This was the crude use of 'branding' in savage times.

More humane and commercial use of 'branding' was leveraged in ancient times by the traders who used to trade in spices, food, clothes and decorative products. They used to Brand their products with their names or the name of their firms. It was then the era of 'trader brands'. Over time some countries also started enjoying respect for the quality of their products fetching them a premium. With it the phenomenon of what is today called

'Geographical brands' came into existence. Thus the 'country brands' and the 'trader brands' co-existed for a long time.

In known history, one of the oldest known brands is 'Staffelter Hof'. Wine has been sold under this brand ever since 862 AD and it continues even today. By 1266, English bakers were required by law to put a specific symbol on each product they sold.

The modern discipline of Brand Management is believed to have started with a famous memo at Procter & Gamble by Neil H. McElroy. In 1931, while he was working on P&G's Camay Brand of soap, he wrote a famous 3-page company memo that laid out the principles of modern Brand Management. He suggested that companies should create marketing teams dedicated to each brand as if it were a separate business. This system was later adopted by most US consumer product companies.

True and exponential development of the area of 'Brand Management' in the market place and within the companies happened in the 20th Century especially after the advent of media in terms of newspapers and radio.

The advent of Television brought in a manifold expansion of the 'Brand World' and it continues to this day. With digital revolution a paradigm shift is underway where the 24*7 reaching out to the customer has become possible and where the customer is far more empowered to choose content. Brands are now ubiquitous and we are now living in an era of 'Brand Clutter'. From advent of the 'Brand' to 'Brand Clutter' has been a long journey much of it happening in the last century.

Beyond the companies today the 'power of the Brand Management' is being harnessed by Non-Profit Organizations, Governments and individuals also. Campaigns to increase tourism into the country like 'Malaysia – Truly Asia' or 'Australia- feels like love' are uses of Brand Management by Governments. Similarly Celebrities and Politicians now hire advertising agencies to create and manage their image in society. The era of 'Social Brands' has come to stay.

4) **Why should Brands exist in this world?**

Brands can't exist in this world unless the producer and the customer both gain something from the existence of the brand. The question is what does each of them gain from the existence of the

Brand? The gains for each are listed here,

a) The gains for the producer;

- If the Brand exists, the product can be traced to its owner and the owner can thus legally own it. Thus the Brand serves as the mark for 'identification of ownership'. Brand here functions as a legal entity.

- **If the producer produces good quality products, he can be rewarded by the customer in terms of repeat purchase and higher margins only if the customer can trace the product back to its producer. Brand enables this to happen. The Brand thus serves as a vehicle to ensure a 'performance reward' to the producer**

- Even when two products are technically similar, 'Differentiation' can be brought in by the producers by adding 'intangible psychological value' into the product. For example, a Brand like Mercedes stands for 'status'. This 'standing for status' is not a phenomenon of nature, it has been consciously created by the producer. The Brand thus makes possible adding of intangible value into the product for differentiation and value enhancement.

- **Brand for the producer is also a form of property in today's world. Consumer marketing companies like Coco-Cola today own much of their property in the form of 'Brand value'. If you look at the property of such companies the**

Brand value of their brands is many times over the value of their tangible assets like land, buildings and equipment. Brand thus is a form of property that can be owned by the producer.

- Brand also is a Strategic asset. The producer can use the value of brands he owns as a currency in merger and acquisition process. Thus Brand is a strategic entity often deployed as a 'strategic and economic currency'.

b) The gains for the customer are;

- The customer is able to identify the producer of the product and based upon the past experience and public reputation of the producer, the customer can make an informed purchase of 'whether to buy a Brand or not'. The Brand thus enables a customer to make a 'buy' or a 'not buy' decision by reducing 'purchase risk'.

- **The customer is assured of a 'level of quality' when he buys a known Brand and hence he can make a good decision on 'how much to pay for what'. The Brand thus provides him with a tool of evaluation of worth of products.**

- The customer in addition to objective product quality also consumes values and images associated with the product when he buys the product as a brand. The existence of 'Brand' thus enables a customer to consume intangible value built into the product.

- **The Brand because it is a legally owned entity also enables the customer to take recourse to legal** remedy in case of dissatisfaction with the product or the company. The Brand thus is a legal entity at the service of the customer.

- The existence of Brand enables the customer to become a 'loyal customer' and correspondingly benefit from 'loyalty programmes'. The customer can thus enter into a more benefitting and relational engagement with the company rather than be limited to a short term transactional engagement with the company.

5) **Which are the World's Top Ten Brands today?**

Every year surveys are done to find out which are the World's top ten brands for that year. The surveys are done by many companies and everyone comes out with its own list of top ten. One such list of

World's top ten brands for the year 2015 is placed below.

Most surveys create the 'top ten' list based upon the 'money value' of a brand. The 'money value' of the brand refers to the amount of money you would get if the Brand was to be sold off today. Some companies use non-monetary factors like 'customer trust' or 'social respect' or 'reputation', however such approaches are not popular.

Given below is 'Interbrand's' list of top ten global brands for the year 2015,

Rank	Brand	Worth in $ Billions
1	Apple	170
2	Google	120
3	Coca-Cola	78
4	Microsoft	67

5	IBM	65
6	Toyota	49
7	Samsung	45
8	GE	42
9	McDonald's	38
10	Amazon	37

Source: Interbrand

6) **Do leading brands remain leading brands for long or does the top ten Brand list keep changing every year?**

The list of 'leading' brands keeps changing every year in every country and also globally. Given the intense competition in the market place it is not easy to continue for long in the top ten Brand list at the level of a country or globally.

7) Which are the leading global brands that have continued to be the 'leading' brands for the longest time?

There has been a long term study to find out which leading global brands have continued to be the 'leading global brands' for the longest time. It is a study conducted by Thomas Wurster, BCG published in 1987. It is a study for the time period of 1925-1985. According to this study, the below given list of brands have continued to be 'leading global brands' across the time period of 1925-1985,

Product	Leading Brand in 1925	Current Position in 1985
Pipe Tobacco	Prince Albert	Leader
Razors	Gillette	Leader
Sewing Machines	Singer	Leader
Shirts	Manhattan	No. 5

Shortening	**Crisco**	Leader
Soap	**Ivory**	Leader
Soup	**Campbell**	Leader
Tea	**Lipton**	Leader
Tyres	**Goodyear**	Leader
Toothpaste	**Colgate**	No. 2

Source – Thomas S Wurster, "The Leading Brands: 1925-1985," Perspectives, BCG, 1987

8) **Has there been a study of what has been the 'Age' of World's leading brands?**

Yes there was a study to find out the 'Age' of world's leading brands. Leo Bogart and Charles Lehman came out with a research in 1973 which studied the 'Age' of then prevailing world's leading brands. The study undertook an 'Age' profiling or leading 4923 brands at the time of the study. The study concluded with findings given here,

Age of the Brand		Percentage of 4,923 Brands Mentioned
Over 100	years	10
75 to 99	years	26
50 to 24	years	28
25 to 49	years	04
15 to 24	years	04
Under 14	years	03

Source- Adapted from Leo Bogart and Charles Lehman, What Makes a Brand Name Familiar? Journal of Marketing Research February 1973, PP. 17-22

Thus only 10% of the world's leading brands then could survive more than 100 years and only 3% could reach the 'world's leading brand list' in less than 15 years.

9) **What are the various 'types of Brands'?**
Brands can be divided into 'types' based on a variety of criteria. One such

classification is given here with examples for each type,

a. **Product Brands**
   Product brands are the Brands under which a single product is being sold. E.g. Liril (soap) and Coke (cola drink)

b. **Product Category Brands**
   Product Category Brands are the Brands under which a range of products in broadly the same category are sold.
   Some examples of it are; Lux (Soap, Shampoo) and Maggi (Noodles, Ketchup)

c. **Corporate Brand**
   Corporate Brands are Brands where the name of the company (or organization) is used to sell most or all of the products of the company (or the organization).

E.g. Hitachi (Air Conditioners, Refrigerators) and General Electric (Medical Equipment, Railway Engines, Air craft Engines)

d. Collective Brands

   Collective Brands are the Brands which are not owned by an individual or an organization but are owned by a 'group of individuals, a group of organizations' or by the Government. Destination brands include; Tourism Brands created for increasing tourism, Co-operative Brands created by community co-operates like Amul, Craft community brands like 'Hand made in India' and Geographical Brands like 'Basmati' (for Rice) owned by Government of India

e. **Private Labels**

   Private Labels are the brands which are owned by a Retailer and sold in his own shop. The Retailer may use his Store name or invent a new name to create a Private Label. E.g. Marks and Spencer Brands sold in Marks and Spencer store is a Private Label. John Miller sold in the retail store 'Pantaloon' is also a Private Label. Private Labels are created by the Retail store to offer the customer an affordable alternative to costly brands, appealing to the cost conscious customer.

f. **Designer Brands**

   Designer Brands are the brands owned by the Designer and generally the Brand name is the same as the name of the Designer. E.g. Armani, Versace

g. **Social Brands**

   Social Brands are the Brands created and owned by Individuals or Organizations without any product to sell. Social Brands are created to advance a purpose, create a positive image for professional benefits or for personal fame.

10) **Why are Private labels created by Retail stores?**

Private Labels are created by Retail stores to offer a customer low price options compared to established Brands. Private Labels also offer the Retailer a higher margin compared to company Brands. Strong Private Labels also provide the Retailer a higher bargaining power in negotiations with the company. E.g. Gap, John Miller, Pantaloons, Marks and Spencer are all examples of private labels.

11) **What is the story of the infamous launch of the 'New Coke'? Why is it so significant in the area of Brand Management?**

Coke and Pepsi were fighting close in the US market. In the context, Coke commissioned research to find out how in terms of 'taste' and 'Brand' can Coke increase its lead over Pepsi.

Researchers gave customers bottles filled with Coke and Pepsi without labels on them and asked them in a blind test to rate the taste. Customers in blind tests rated Pepsi as having better taste than Coke. The same experiment was repeated with the same customers but now with Brands mentioned on the bottles. This time customers liked the taste of Coke more than Pepsi. It meant something surprising that even something 'objective' as taste is not as objective as we think. The effect of the

Brand is so pervasive that Customers change their 'taste preference' with presence or absence of the Brand.

Consumer Preference Tests on Coke & Pepsi

	Blind Tests	Open Branded Test
Prefer Pepsi	51%	23%
Prefer Coke	44%	65%
Equal/cannot say	5%	12%

In the next step of the experiment, different 'tastes' were experimented with under conditions of blind testing. Finally one taste which under blind testing conditions, customers liked more than Pepsi was chosen to be the next 'taste' for a 'New Coke'.

The company launched the 'New Coke' with a better taste and supported by a huge advertising campaign.

Unfortunately the launch failed. People who liked the 'taste' under blind test conditions no longer were ready to buy it. Customers were so attached to the 'Old Coke as it was' that they refused to patronize the new Coke. Sales dropped and the company was forced to relaunch the 'Old Coke'.

The significance of this incidence is twofold. One that the power of the Brand is so high that even an otherwise felt objective issue like 'taste' is influenced by the Brand and two that in case of Coke, the customer's decision to purchase was based less on taste, calories, nutrition and was more based on emotional issues related to Coke. Customer's decision to buy here was depending on subjective and psychological aspects and not on objective issues like price, taste, availability and so on. On the whole it

enunciates aloud, 'the power of the Brand'.

12) **What has been the journey of Brand Management like over the last 50 years?**
Brand Management has grown in terms of significance and in terms of financial spends over the last 50 years. Brand Management today is one of the most critical functions of consumer marketing organizations. Industrial product organizations also have now climbed the Brand-wagon and they too create brands. Since today the Brand-spend especially for consumer marketing companies is very large, the return on Brand-spend is a strong determinant of returns on market-spend and that inturn is a strong determinant of the corporate return on investment. This linkage of RoI on Brand Management determining to a great extent the Corporate RoI (in case of consumer marketing companies) has

immensely enhanced the significance of Brand Management.

13) Is Brand Management a mature discipline or is it still evolving?

Brand Management is not a mature discipline like Economics or Mathematics where there is a consensus with regard to the 'fundamentals of the discipline'. The controversy begins with 'What is a Brand?', there is no consensus on the definition of the word 'Brand'. The area of Brand Management is an evolving area and so every thinker coins his terms. Every book you read you will come across two new terms never heard before. The good part however is in the last five years in academia and in practice we are converging on some consensus with regard to fundamental terms in the area of Brand Management.

14) **Is Brand Management different from Advertising?**

Yes, Brand Management is different from Advertising. Advertising is a part of Brand Management. Brand Management comprises of areas like Brand strategy, Brand valuation, Brand creation, Brand maintenance and others. Advertising is only one of the tools (in addition to public relations and events) that Brand Management uses for the purpose of creating and maintaining brands. Areas within Brand Management like Brand strategy, Brand valuation have nothing to do with advertising.

15) **What do we mean by customer profiling?**

Every citizen in society is not our customer. Our products are bought for a particular purpose by a particular group of people. It is necessary here to know the 'profile' of this group who buys our product or can potentially buy our product. Customer profiling is an attempt to create a 'profile' of our customers or potential customers, so that we can customize our products and Brand Management efforts.

16) **What do we mean by demographic and psychographic charactersticks?**

Every person can be described and understood by using the concept of demographic and psychographic charactersticks. Demographic charactersticks include issues like age, gender, education, occupation and income whereas Psychographic charactersticks include issues like Personality, values, beliefs, preferences, relationship patterns, social image, self-image etc.

Demographic and Psychographic charactersticks both put together give us

a reasonable profile of the individual. It is by using on a social scale the demographic and psychographic charactersticks of our customer group and potential customer group, that we are able to create our Products and our Brand Campaign (including advertisements).

17) **Can you sell a bad product using good advertisements?**

Obviously not. A good Brand is created owing to two factors. The objective set of reasons include product quality, price, availability, retail experience and after sales service. The subjective set of reasons includes Brand Image, Brand Personality, Retail Experience, Company's Reputation and so on. Good advertising may lead the customer to buy the product once but if the product fails, no amount of good advertising can make him buy the product again. Not to mention that he spreads a negative word of mouth both offline and online and influences others not to buy the product. Thus a bad product no matter how good the advertising is.

18) **How is a 'Brand' protected in terms of 'Intellectual Property Rights'?**

The Brand is protected as a 'trade mark' under the Intellectual property Rights law. The logo, the Brand name can be protected under this law. Registering a Brand name provides security for future but there is no security if some one else has been using the same Brand name in the same territory and the same product category. In such a case even though you have registered a Brand name you can lose it in the courts.

19) **What is the process for getting your Brand protected as a trade mark?**

First step is to arrive at a Brand name and a logo (if you so wish, it is optional). Step two is to go to a trade mark registration office and fill up a 'search request form'. Within a few days you will get a 'search report' which tells you if or not this name you seek to register is available or has already been taken. Once the search report gives a go ahead you can fill up the registration form and attach five visiting cards with the Brand name and Logo (if it exists) and pay the fees.

20) **Do you have to make a separate application for each country or is the protection offered to a Brand as a trademark is global?**

Brand name protection is offered on a product category and territorial basis. For example if 'Cool and Blue' is your Brand name and you are selling Ice-creams then you may be given Brand name protection only for that product category. Any other producer can come in your District and start using 'Cool and Blue' Brand name to sell Bicycles, you can't stop him. If you wish to have protection in more than one product category for your brand name then you have to move a separate trade mark application for each product category.

21) **Can the trade mark protection be offered on a territorial basis?**

Yes it can be. If there is an instance where the brand name you are using is X and some one else is using the same Brand name X in a different State and both of you are selling the same product then each of you can be given Brand name protection limited to your state. Such territorial (limited) Brand name protection is quite common amongst small shop keepers or traders.

22) What is the concept of a 'Well Known Brand'?

Global Brands like LG, Samsung, Sony, Google, IBM and so on are popular across the world. For protecting their Brand name globally the MNCs who own these global brands have to move trade mark applications in all countries and in all product categories. Should they forget to do it some one in a host country can start mis-using their Brand name to sell his products. To over come this issue the concept of Well-Known Brand has been created whereby the globally popular Brands are deemed protected even if an application is not made in a couple of countries. The concept being that regardless of the application being made or otherwise, in the market these Brands are well-known and so anyone using the same Brand name is into will-full misuse and has to be stopped.

23) **Is it important to study Brand success stories and Brand Failures?**

Yes it is. Brand success stories provide us with a perspective and ideas that have worked in varied contexts and our context may resemble one of the varied contexts we study.

Brand Failures happen broadly on account of two factors; a) Brand related Factors or b) Non-Brand related Factors. A Brand may fail purely out of the company closing down due to labor problems or capital shortage or dispute between owners or just product quality or spare part issues. One has to be careful to see if the Brand failure is owing to Brand factors or non-Brand factors and in our own contexts we have to be vigilant based on our study of Brand failures.

Brand success stories and Brand Failure stories have been elaborately documented and a study of them is an essential preparation for practice of Brand Management.

24) **How does a Brand get created?**

Brand is a collection of associations in the individual's mind. This collection of association gets created because of inputs coming from advertisements, media articles and interviews, event sponsorships by companies, product experience of the individual, retail experience of the individual, word of mouth about the Brand and the company in society (offline and online) and company reputation. All these inputs and experiences get processed in the individual's mind and create a net result we call the Brand. The Brand creation process is depicted here graphically,

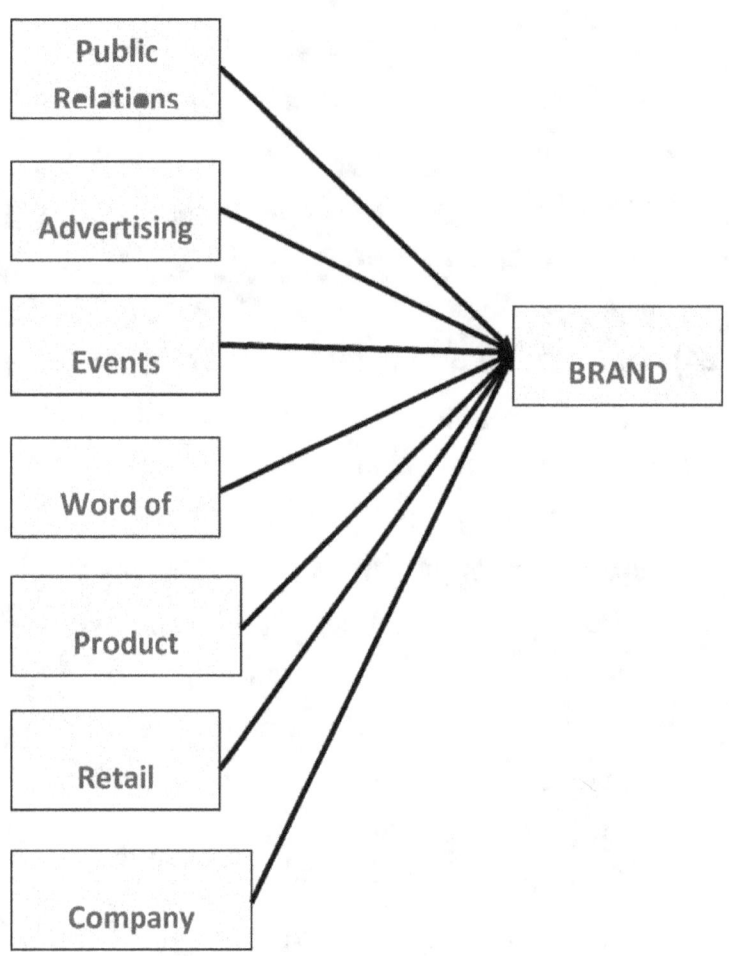

25) What is the Canvas of Brand Management like? What are the major concepts and issues in the area of Brand Management?

Brand Management is an evolving area and a number of 'thematic areas' and 'concepts within each thematic area' have developed within the area of Brand Management.

Tabulated below are these 'themes and concepts' under broad category heads. Each of the themes and concepts tabulated below has been engaged with, in this Book.

```
┌─────────────────────────┐
│    Brand Management     │
└─────────────────────────┘
              │
              ▼
```

Table 1

General areas and concepts	Brand creation	Brand maintenance
History of the brand	Brand Strategy and S-T-P	Brand Tactics
Legal aspects of the brand	Brand Architecture	Brand alternation
Types of brands	Brand Positioning	Brand rejuvenation
Brand Culture	Brand Identity	Brand extension
Celebrity Endorsement	Corporate Identity	Brand re-launching
Brand Failures	The tactical mix	Co-branding
Brand commoditization	The creative mix	Cause related

		branding
Quality led brand	The media mix	Brand promotion
Crisis campaigns	The event mix	
Thematic Brand campaigns	Logo and Mascots	
Brand and controversy	Brand Aesthetics	
Empty brands	Return on Campaign	

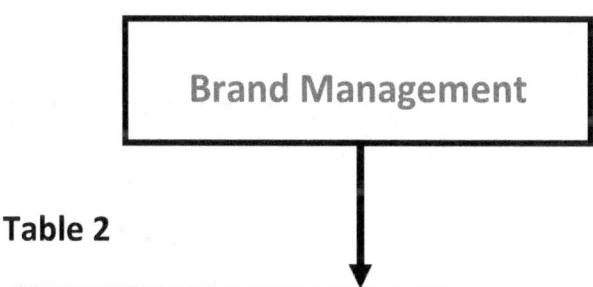

Table 2

The Brand anatomy and psychology	Brand Management : Specialty Application	The Brand valuation
Brand	Cult brands	Sales

Awareness		method
Brand comprehension	Collective brands	Premium method
Brand Preference	Ingredient branding	Market capitalization method
Brand usage	Industrial product brands	Profit method
Brand loyalty	Brand Management for SME	Customer oriented method
Brand Experience	Brand Management for Non-Profits	Strategic premium
Brand Image	Brand Management for the Government	Brand and portfolio evaluation
Brand Personality	Brand Management for Individuals	Merger and acquisition valuations
Self image-	Managing	Return on

Brand image congruence	global brands	Brand Management
Brand ethics	PR Led or Event led Brand Management	
Brand Identity	Experiential Brand Management	
Brand Essence	Digital Brand Management	

Within every Brand is a product, but not every product is a brand

David Ogilvy

BRAND MANAGEMENT: FUNDAMENTAL CONCEPTS

Brands are decision-making shortcuts in a world of people like you, looking for shortcuts
Harry Beckwith, Selling the Invisible

26) What is Brand Awareness?

Brand awareness refers to, if or not you have 'aware' about the existence of a given brand. Brand awareness is a state, either you are aware of the Brand or you are not.

However if you are aware of the Brand then there is a 'range of awareness' possible and you may have awareness of a particular type. The range of awareness includes; a) Top of the mind awareness (TOM) b) Unaided awareness (UA) c) Aided awareness (AA). Top of the mind awareness refers to the first name that comes to mind when one is asked to think of brands in a particular product segment. Unaided awareness refers to

the set of Brand names that one is able to recollect without aid from anyone. Aided awareness refers to the Brand names that you are able to recollect only when help is extended.

Companies have to strive to ensure that their brands enjoy either TOM or UA. Unless you are in these two categories, chances of doing good on sales are very less.

27) What is Brand Comprehension?

Brand comprehension refers to the knowledge one has related to any given brand. It includes knowledge about; a) the products being sold under the Brand b) values the Brand represents c) the social class or segment to which the Brand caters d) the brand personality and the associations one has in the mind related to the Brand e) the company that makes the Brand and its reputation.

28) What is Brand Preference?

Brand Preference refers to the overall liking one has related to a given Brand. Brand Preference develops after Brand awareness and Brand comprehension. Brand preference may or may not result in purchase. Between Brand preference and Brand purchase (Usage) stand affordability and availability.

29) What is Brand Usage?

Brand Usage refers to the customer actually using the brand. In normal language it would be called sales. Brand Usage happens only if after Brand preference, affordability and availability support transition from Brand preference to Brand usage.

30) What is Brand Loyalty?

Brand Loyalty refers to the repeated usage of a brand. Brand loyalty is the result of the customer being highly satisfied with Brand usage. The customer with high Brand loyalty also becomes the Brand ambassador for the Brand he is delighted with. Brand Loyalty thus has elements of repeat purchase and Brand ambassadorship.

31) **What is Consumer's Brand Adoption Process?**

The customer's Brand adoption process is the process that starts with Brand awareness and ends with Brand loyalty. The following are the steps in the process,

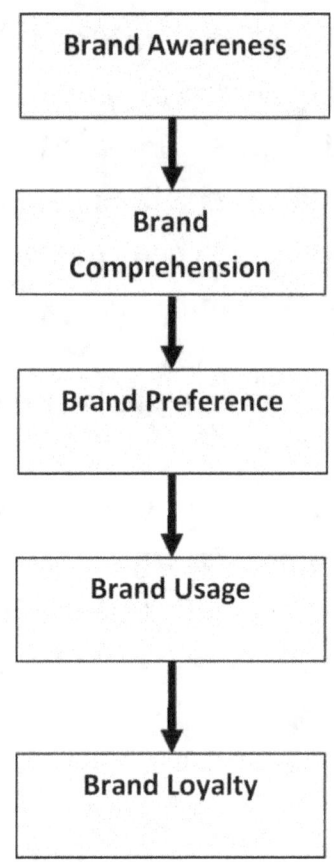

Consumer's Brand Adoption Process

32) **What is Segmentation?**

Segmentation is the act of dividing the society into groups or segments based upon some criteria like income, age, gender, occupation, education psychological preference etc. One can and mostly one does, use more than one criteria for the purpose of segmentation.

Segmentation is necessary because it is very difficult to create a product or an advertisement which will appeal to all the groups in the society. Take an example, if you are selling chocolates inevitably your group of interest is going to be children. You will hence create your products and advertisements with this group or segment in your mind. Here what has happened is you have divided the society on the basis of age and you have focused your attention on the group called children. Similarly if you selling a Mercedes, you have to divide the society on the basis of income and then focus your attention upon the high income group. Without segmentation we don't know whom to please and without it sales and profits are too low. Some product segments categories and the most common criteria used for segmentation for them are listed here,

Product Category	Criteria for Segmentation
Toys	Age
Cars	Income
Soaps	Income, Personality
After Shave	Gender, Age, Personality

33) **What is Targeting?**

Segmentation is the act of dividing the society into segments (groups) based on some criteria. At the end of segmentation, we have before us a picture of society divided into groups. Targeting is the act of selecting any of these 'groups or segments' for focus. Targeting helps us to arrive at a clear target and so we know the demographic and psychographic profile of our target and we can focus our limited resources and efforts hence on to please this target segment.

Take an example. Say a company is selling toys and for the purpose it divides society into segments based upon age. Then the company has to select a segment for focus. This act of selecting a segment is called targeting. So if toys are consumed in the age group of 1-10 years then the company may choose to focus on girl child toys in the age group of 5-10 years and in the low income segment in the said age group. This will define for the company the segment to be targeted, girls in the age group of 5-10 years belonging to low income and middle income families. Once the target segment is decided, the company goes for a detailed psychological study of the

target segment to understand it better for product creation and advertising.

34) **What is Positioning?**

Once targeting is done, the target segment is studied in details both demographically and psychographically. The perceptual space of the target segment is studied to ascertain how each competing Brand is placed in the perceptual space of the target customers. The Brand then has to find a place for itself in the mind of the target customers vis-à-vis the competition. Once conceptually clear about the place one wants to be in the target customer's mind space, product, price, advertising etc. is geared to establish the Brand in the mind-space as desired. This act of placing our Brand in the perceptual space of the target customer vis-à-vis the competition is called positioning.

Let us continue with the last example. Let us say the Toy company is clear it has to focus on 5-10 year low and middle income girls then the company has to decide with what idea, feeling or value the Brand wishes to get associated. Every Brand is associated with some idea or feeling or value, Mercedes is associated with status and Liril with 'lime freshness'. Similarly our Brand can get associated with 'affordability', 'quality', 'status' or some other value. This value or idea is called the positioning attribute and in our language we say, the Brand is positioned on X (here say quality). If this is concluded, the product has to be manufactured as a high quality high warranty product and the advertisement has to highlight the 'quality' aspect of it.

Segmentation, Targeting and Positioning are three steps of a single sequence, often referred to as S-T-P.

35) What is Brand Experience?

The consumer experiences the Brand by experiencing it at every touch point. The touch points include, consuming the product, experiencing the communication of the Brand, participating in events sponsored by the company or where the company is participating and retail experience related to the Brand. The sum total of these experiences in the consumer's mind creates what is called the consumer's 'Brand experience'.

36) What is Brand Image?

Brand Image is the image the individual has about the Brand in his mind. One can see the Brand as a 'premium brand' or a 'value for money brand' or as a 'designer brand' or as a 'cult brand'. One can view the brand as being very sophisticated or rustic, young or old, contemporary or retro. One can have any image of the Brand in his mind. This image in the individual's mind is called the Brand Image.

Versace has the image of being a high end, creative designer Brand while Toyota has the Brand image of being a value for money good quality reliable product, while Harley Davidson has the Brand image of being an offbeat, iconoclastic and macho Brand.

37) **What is Brand Personality?**

We all have 'associations' regarding Brands in our minds. Does that mean we think of Brands just as we think about people? Not always but at times we do. We do think about Brands at times as though the Brand was a person. Brand personality refers to the personality of this person.

Brand personality hence refers to the personality the Brand would have had, had it been a person. Brand personality research tells us that people more often than not think of Brands (unconsciously ofcourse) as a person and they do attribute a personality to the Brand.

Brand personality as an area has been extensively researched by Jennifer Aaker. She has shown that the five most common attributes people associate with (or evaluate with) Brand personality are; Ruggedness, Sophistication, Sincerity, Competence and Excitement.

38) What is Corporate Identity?

Corporate Identity refers to the visual Identity created in the individual's mind when he is exposed to 'visuals' related to the company which includes; letter head, visiting cards, all communication visuals, retail visuals, transport visuals, packaging and so on). The name and the logo plays a very important part in creating the Corporate Identity. Advertising companies create a 'manual' called the 'corporate identity manual' to make sure every time the logo or any other visual is printed it comes out to be exactly the same. The corporate identity manual is given to the printer or producer.

Some companies have a logo with only a name and some have a logo constituted of a name and a symbol. Some good logo(s) are given here,

39) What is Brand Identity?

Brand Identity is defined in two broad ways. One definition is the visual definition of Brand Identity and second is the visual cum ideational definition of Brand Identity.

The visual definition says, Brand Identity is created by the name, logo, forms, colors, typography, model types, packaging, transport graphics, retail graphics, activity graphics etc. related to the Brand. Here the Brand Identity is constituted of associations derived from

the visual aspect of the Brand and one can associate Brand Identity with being Youthful, Colorful, Reliable, Stable and so on.

The second definition is a 'visual and ideational' definition of Brand Identity and it includes both ideational and visual elements with which the Brand is associated. Here the ideational associations created by communication are also taken into account and so the Brand Identity can be understood to be, Classy, Rich, Success, Sensuous, Exciting, Adventurous, Serious and so on. This second definition comes from Kapferer's approach to Brand identity which includes both visual and ideational elements.

40) **What is Brand Essence?**
Brand Essence is the unchanging core of the brand. It is an idea or a value at the

heart of the brand. Thus advertisements within a campaign keep changing every month. The campaign itself changes every 3 months. The identity can change once every 3-5 years whereas the Essence would change hardly once in 10 years. It is the most enduring element in the brand.

For example, if Wal-Mart stands for 'economy and savings' this essence of the Brand continues across decades. Although advertising campaigns may change every three months, no campaign can portray Wal-Mart as a premium product's retailer or a place where you go for an 'experience of luxury' (like in case of Harrods). Thus campaigns will change every 3-6 months, the colors used by Wal-Mart in its communication may change once in 5 years but the Brand Essence continues across decades unless Wal-Mart decides to change its philosophy at its heart.

41) **What is Brand Psychology?**

The Brand essentially is a psychological entity in the mind of the individual. The study of the entire psychological process involved in Brand creation, Brand maintenance, Brand interpretation and Brand evaluation that happens in the mind of the individual, is referred to as Brand psychology.

Naturally there are varied schools of psychology and so there are correspondingly varied approaches and explanations in the area of Brand Psychology. Since much of Brand processing is unconscious in nature, Psychoanalysis offers a very promising approach in the area of Brand psychology.

42) What is E-Branding?

E-branding is a term liberally used to connote, Electronic Branding or Internet branding or digital branding. The advent of internet and mobile communication has altered the way people use media and where they spend most of their free and working time. Using internet, mobile communication as media vehicles and creating communication content for these media vehicles for a Brand purpose, constitutes what is termed as E-branding. Mass emailing, communication on social media and optimization of one's website are some of the most common measures in the area of E-Branding.

43) What is Celebrity Endorsement?

Celebrities are often used to create Brands. The use of a celebrity helps create a Brand in a short time and in a matter of few weeks, create a familiarity, trust and a liking for the Brand. Given the time gain many companies go for celebrity endorsement although it is costly. Celebrity endorsement is an important tactical decision involving large amount of financial resources.

44) Why does Celebrity Endorsement work?

Celebrity endorsement works on the principle of 'transfer of associations'. The associations one has with regard to the celebrity are transferred onto the Brand the celebrity endorses. Most common associations that are transferred are, familiarity, trust, liking, ruggedness, excitement, reliability, sophistication, competence, beauty, goodness and omnipotence.

45) Are some celebrities over used or wrongly used for endorsement?

Yes it is indeed so. A celebrity should be used for endorsing a Brand only when a fit is found between the Brand and the Celebrity. You can't have a 'pastry soft celebrity' endorsing a Harley Davidson or Old spice. Similarly you can't have a physically weak celebrity with many diseases endorsing Nike.

46) Is there something called Celebrity Dependence?

Yes it is. Brands which use too much of Celebrities like Lux over time become dependent on Celebrity endorsement and even if they wish to they find it difficult to get out of it. Celebrity endorsement is good for Brand launch and Brand rejuvenation but not for everyday Brand Management (this is true for most but not all brands). Using celebrity endorsement for everyday Brand management is a costly addiction.

47) **Is there a theoretical model to help us choose the right Celebrity for endorsing our brand?**

Yes there is. There is a fourteen point model (and other models also) which help find the right celebrity for the right brand based on fourteen parameters. All these celebrity selection models, basically find a fit between the celebrity's gender, age, path of success, personality, values and (on the other side with) the Brand positioning, Brand Personality, Brand Associations and Brand Essence.

48) **What is Brand Aesthetics?**

Aesthetics is the science of beauty. It is the science of color, form, typography, composition, symmetry, proportion, feelings and human depiction. Aesthetics when it is at the service of Brand Management is called Brand Aesthetics.

It deals with the visual aspect of Brand Management.

49) **Where is the application of Brand aesthetics in practice?**
Brand Aesthetics is applied to the entire visual aspect of Brand Management. If you see an advertisement in a magazine and you don't like it, perhaps Brand Aesthetics has not been practiced well. May be the colors are not right or perhaps there is too much material in the advertisement or may be the fonts used are not right.

Let us take an example using one element of Brand Aesthetics which is Fonts (Typography). Given below is caption of Intel (Intel Inside) in different Fonts. Isn't it amply clear that right choice of fonts is so essential to Brand Management?

If you were to color these different fonts with different colors new combinations for choices would emerge.

Intel Inside

Intel Inside

Intel Inside

Intel Inside

Intel Inside

intel inside

Intel Inside

intel inside

50) **How do you learn 'Brand aesthetics' since it is not a standard part of curriculum in most B-Schools?**

Brand Aesthetics is the typically the domain of professionals in the area of Graphics, Fashion or Design. Brand Management as it is taught in B-Schools doesn't address this issue much and it constitutes a deficit in the training of

Brand managers. In dealing with the advertising agency, one of the areas where Brand managers are not able to articulate their likes or dislike is the area of Brand Aesthetics. Also the return on Brand spend can be increased manifold if Brand managers are empowered with the knowledge of Brand Aesthetics. Brand Aesthetics can be learnt in training programmes being offered by specialized Institutes or from training Consultants.

Your Brand is what other people say about you when you're not in the room
Jeff Bezos, Amazon.com

PART II   THE BRAND CAMPAIGN

A great Brand is a story that's never completely told. A Brand is a metaphorical story that connects with something very deep —a fundamental appreciation of mythology- Stories create the emotional context people need to locate themselves in a larger experience

Scott Bedbury, Starbucks

Branding *adds spirit and a soul to what would otherwise be a robotic, automated, generic price-value proposition. If branding is ultimately about the creation of human meaning, it follows logically that it is the humans who must ultimately provide it*

David Aaker

CREATING THE BRAND

Unless you have absolute clarity of what your Brand stands for, everything else is irrelevant
Mark Baynes, Global CMO, Kellogg

51) What is a Brand Strategy? How is it arrived at?

Strategy that governs the creation and maintenance of the Brand in the competitive situation is referred to as Brand Strategy. Brand Strategy is arrived at essentially like any other strategy is arrived at, by arriving at a match between opportunities in the environment and competencies inside the organization. Competition analysis, core competence analysis and emerging future changes are some of the factors which have to be factored in while arriving at a Brand Strategy. For example if competitive analysis suggests there is an opportunity in rapidly growing luxury segment and you have a core competence in luxury marketing then it is worthwhile to create a Brand in that Segment.

52) **How is the Brand strategy related to the corporate strategy?**

The overall strategy guiding a company is called its Corporate Strategy. Every function (marketing, finance, human resources and operations) makes congruent its functional strategy to the corporate strategy. Thus market strategy is congruent to the Corporate strategy and Brand Strategy is congruent to the marketing strategy (marketing department is a part of the company and Brand Management is a part of marketing). The linkage is schematically depicted below,

For example if the corporate strategy is to create a turnover of one billion dollars from a particular product segment in a given country in a period of 3 years, you can't have a market strategy which goes for premium products, you have to go for mass products. Once the decision to go for mass products is made at the market strategy level, at the level of Brand strategy we have no choice but to position our Brand as a mass brand on attributes like affordability, quality, happiness, reliability and so on. We don't have a choice to create a 'status brand'.

53) **What does the Brand Strategy deal with? What are the issues related to each component of Brand Strategy?**

Brand strategy deals with issues of,
   a) Brand Architecture
   b) Brand Portfolio
   c) Brand Positioning

Brand Architecture

Brand Architecture refers to the relationships between all the brands of the company and the relationships of these brands with the corporate Brand (if any). There are three types of Brand architectures,

   a) Focused
   b) Extended
   c) Hybrid

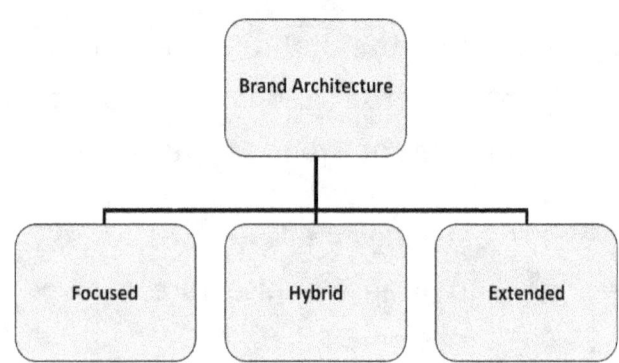

Three Generic types of Brand Architecture

Focused Brand architecture is a situation where the company uses one Brand to sell only one product. Say Coke is used to sell only carbonated drinks. Extended architecture refers to the situation when the company uses the same Brand to sell many products, viz. Samsung is used to sell a variety of products including mobile phones, refrigerators, ovens, washing machines and so on. The Hybrid architecture is an in-between situation where the Brand is used to sell more than one product but not too many products like in case of an Extended architecture.

Every company has to take decisions on what type of architecture it wants to create and each product sector has its own dynamics as to which architecture will work there. Thus in FMCG sector one can find many companies with focused Brand architecture whereas in the Consumer Durables category most companies practice an Extended Brand architecture.

If the purchase decision is driven by psychological issues then focused architecture is generally preferred. If the product is technically complex, of high cost or involves high risk, consumer's prefer tried and tested large company products and so the Extended architecture works better. From cost point of view the Focused Brand architecture is costly to maintain compared to the other two forms of architecture.

The company has to clear from the beginning about the architecture, once the Brand is created, in future if you wish to change the architecture, it may or not be possible to do so, depending on the Brand name and associations related to the Brand.

For example, if you create a Brand called monster.com, in future you can extend it (with great expense ofcourse but yet is possible) into other product areas but if you create a Brand like Jobs.com then you can't extend it in future to any other product category.

Brand Portfolio
In every product category there are 'segments' based upon price, product

features and customer's psychographic charactersticks. For example in the category of cars one can see the segmentation in price terms as given here,

Product Segment	Brand
Affordable	Suzuki Alto
Value for Money	Hyundai Ascent
Quality	Honda City
Status	Mercedes
Experience	Ferrari

Similarly in every product category there is a pyramid like above and the company has to decide which segments to enter with which Brands.

Also a company may be operating in more than one product categories like GE which operates in aviation engines, railway locomotives and medical equipment. The company then has to decide if to use the same Brand/s for all categories or create different Brands for the same. Thus a portfolio of products is sold under a portfolio of Brands. This portfolio of Brands is called Brand Portfolio.

Brand Portfolio to be created in future should be clear to the company at the time of designing the Brand Architecture so that a clear long term strategy without any speed breakers in future, can be arrived at.

Experience
Status
Quality
Value for Money
Affordability

Essential Segments in any Product Category

Brand Positioning

Imagine the mind of the audience as being a space. In this space every Brand the person knows of resides. Each Brand residing in the mind of the person is associated with ideas, feelings and values. Thus every Brand occupies a unique position in the mind space of the audience. This unique existence of the Brand with its associations is called a 'position' and the process of taking the Brand to this 'position' is called Brand positioning.

Brand positioning means what idea, feeling or value the Brand is most strongly associated with in the mind of the audience. Thus when you think of Liril you think of Lime Freshness and when you think of Mercedes you think of status and success. We say in our language that Liril is positioned on the positioning attribute of 'lime freshness' and Mercedes is positioned on the positioning attribute of 'Status and Success'.

The company has to decide whether the Brand is to be positioned in the mind of the audience as a mass market brand, a class market brand, a high quality brand, an innovative design Brand and so on. Two important aspects for positioning are; a) is there a gap where you can enter in the product space you are operating b) can you be among the top three in terms of product performance on whatever idea you wish to position yourself. Equally important is the fact whether or not the company culture is congruent and capable of sustaining the values of the Brand on a long term basis.

Brand Architecture, Brand Portfolio and Brand Positioning are naturally strongly linked to each other as they are parts of the Brand Strategy.

54) What is a Brand Campaign?

The Brand Campaign is a co-ordinated set of measures undertaken inorder to create or maintain a Brand. The Brand Campaign is generally created and managed by the advertising agency which works for the company who owns the Brand.

If a company undertakes measures in a disjointed unsystematic manner to create a Brand, it is not called a Brand campaign. The operative word here is a 'co-ordinated set of measures'. Small and medium scale companies often do one off advertisements or one off event participation and the same doesn't constitute a Brand Campaign. In general, every campaign is on an average of 2-3 months of duration.

55) What are the components of the Brand Campaign?

The Brand Campaign has three main components,

a) Public Relations

b) Advertising

c) Events

Public relations refers to communication done in such a way that the audience is not able to make out that it is a paid communication and so the credibility of that communication is very high. Public Relations includes interviews and articles in Press, Television, Internet and Radio.

Advertising obviously refers to communication where the audience is able to make out that it is a paid communication. It includes advertisements in Press, Television, Internet, Transport communication,

Retail communication and corporate communication.

'Events' includes sponsoring or participating in exhibitions, sports events, film events and so on.

56) **What is 360 degree integrated communication?**
The Brand Campaign combines elements of Public Relations, Advertising and Events to create a systematic way to get in touch with the audience. The idea is to surround the customer 360 degree whether he is inside his home or out of home.

Hence during a Brand Campaign as a part of public relations exercise news articles are printed in newspapers with a particular theme, the same theme is communicated by advertisements released on television, in press, on hoardings and on internet. Events are engaged with where communication with the same theme is being done.

Thus the same thematic communication happens through public relations, advertising and events using a variety of media vehicles to surround the audience 360 with the same thematic communication. This is called a 360 degree integrated communication approach of the Brand campaign.

57) **How is a Brand created or maintained by a company?**
The company generally hires an advertising agency to create or maintain a Brand. Brand is created or maintained by virtue of,

    a) Brand Campaign involving public relations, advertising and events
    b) Word of mouth in society regarding the Brand

c) Product experience of the customer

d) Retail experience of the customer or the potential customer

e) Company reputation

58) What is the process of Brand creation in practice?

In practice, the company has to first select an advertising agency. To do this, the company invites advertising agencies to make a 'pitch' for the account. The advertising agency selected is then given the brief. The brief includes the corporate strategy and the marketing strategy and in the light of it the Brand strategy is evolved in consultation between the company and the advertising agency.

The advertising agency then starts working out a Brand Campaign in the light of competition. The Brand campaign has three components, public relations, advertising and events. The advertising agency comes out with a variety of creative ideas for all the three components of the Brand campaign. The advertising agency then internally discusses the alternatives and in the end comes to two or three alternative Brand Campaigns. The presentation is then made to the company and one Brand Campaign is selected. The collection of creative elements of the Brand campaign is referred to as the Creative Mix.

Each creative has to reach the audience riding on some media vehicle. Media planning comes in here. It is necessary to optimize the selection of media vehicles and the time and frequency of their use inorder to get best returns on the campaign spending. The media planning department of the advertising agency generally does this job. The media plan is also discussed with the company and a decision is taken on it.

The negotiations with the media companies follow and then the communication is released in the media. The media tracking activity is aimed at ensuring that the media vehicle chosen actually releases the communication as contracted.

Detailed analysis of audience response to our Brand campaign is carried out and after the campaign is over a 'campaign returns study' (by any name you call it) is done to ascertain the return on investment of the campaign spending and what short term and long term effects the campaign has had on the Brand Equity. Third party neutral consultants or consulting firms are best placed to do the 'campaign returns study' since they don't have any 'conflict of interest' in the context.

This is the complete process in practice of creating a Brand.

59) **What is a teaser?**

Sometimes a Brand campaign starts with a 'teaser'. Teaser is a phase where the Brand campaign starts but the communication doesn't reveal the name of the brand. Curiosity is created in the minds of the customer with enigmatic and intriguing copy or visual. 'It is coming' guess who? Is the theme of the communication. The teaser is an appetizer for the real Brand campaign.

The teaser gets a much higher customer involvement and they start thinking about which Brand it would be and often it leads to a conversation among people. After a week or two the campaign reveals which Brand is being referred to and then the real campaign starts.

60) How does the Brand get actually created? Is everything in the hands of the company or the advertising agency?
The Brand gets created in the mind of the audience, under the influence of; a) Brand campaign done by the company b) customer's product experience c) word of mouth about the brand in society d) retail experience of the customer e) company's reputation.

Thus the Brand gets created partly owing to communication and partly owing to objective factors like price, product features, product quality, availability and after sales service. Only Brand campaign is the factor which is partly in the control of the company and the advertising agency, rest of the factors are not in their control.

The process by which the Brand gets created in the mind of the audience is schematically depicted here including which activity of the Brand campaign is to be done by whom,

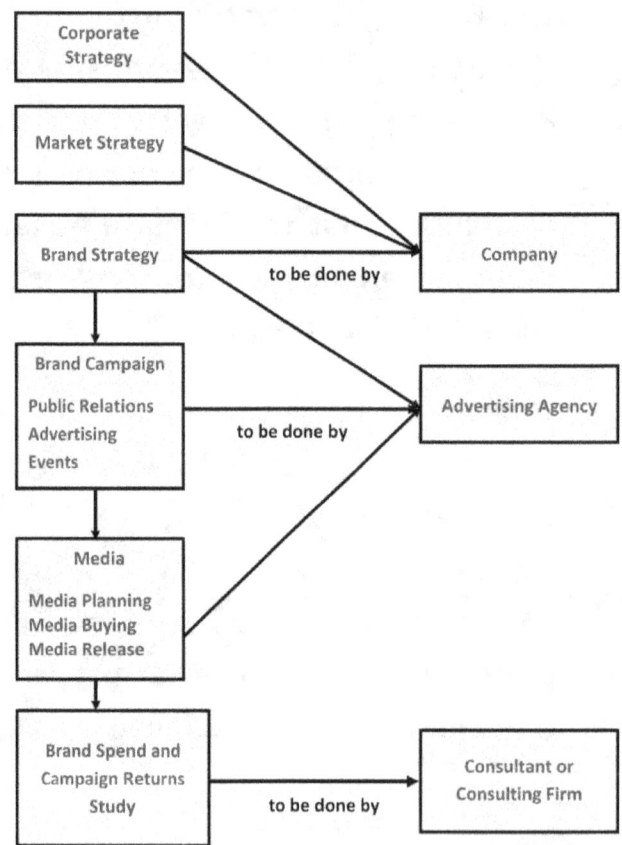

61) What are departments within an Advertising Agency? What are their functions?

Traditionally the departments within the Advertising Agency have been; a) Client servicing b) Strategy c) Creative d) Public Relations e) Media and f) Events. With increasing specialization and outsourcing, new departments like digital marketing have come up within advertising agencies while areas like Public relations, Media Planning and Events are now outsourced to specialized companies.

Client Servicing

The Client Servicing professionals are the ones who interact with the client and who are the bridge between the company and the advertising agency on a day to day basis. They are generally junior level professionals in the advertising agency.

Strategy

The strategy team deals with Brand Strategy. It involves senior professionals in the agency. It provides overall direction to key accounts. Some agencies don't have this department rather they have senior professionals who are called key accounts head and they provide the strategic direction to that account (brand) The strategy team provides guidelines for the creative department. Often they do or commission research for a clearer understanding before giving a brief to the creative department. Professionals in this department are mostly with a management background.

Creative

The creative department is responsible for making creative for the Brand campaign. The creative team deals with the visual part and the copy writing part of the Brand campaign. They create visual material, write-ups, scripts, advertisements, corporate films and similar material. Professionals of the creative department mostly come with a fine arts, applied arts or design background.

Media

The media department deals with 'media planning' and 'media release'. The media team selects media vehicles should be used for reaching out to the target audience and how much of each vehicle should be used and on which day and time. Professionals of this department mostly come with a management background with special interest in journalism or media. Many advertising agencies now don't have this department in the agency and outsource this function of 'media planning', 'media release' and 'media tracking' to specialized companies.

Public Relations

Public Relations professionals are generally with a prior background in journalism and are expected to enjoy a good rapport with Editors in various media companies. The public relations team creates material for articles, cover stories, interviews and also ensures that it (the material created) features in leading media vehicles. Like Media, the Public Relations function has now got extremely specialized and so most advertising agencies now outsource this function.

Events
Professionals of this area generally come with a prior experience in event Management. Most advertising agencies

now outsource event Management. Some Advertising agencies have created subsidiary companies which do event Management for them and also for independent clients. The event management team plans and executes the 'event' part of the Brand campaign. The team has to oversee event participation, event sponsorship, on road activities, institutional activities, residential society activities and so on. Creatives needed for events are supplied by the creative team of the advertising agency.

62) How should a company select an Advertising agency?

Selection of an advertising agency is a critical decision in the Brand Management process. Most companies are not clear about it and so learn it the hard way with heavy costs. Some of the points to consider in selection of an advertising agency are given here,

a) Select an agency that matches the size of your account. If you are going to spend USD 1000 on your campaign and the agency turnover is USD 1 Million, your account is too small for the agency and the best professionals of the agency will be working on the bigger accounts and not on your account. Select the right size.

b) Select an agency that has proven in your area of business. Some agencies are good in creating Industrial brands and some are good in creating Consumer brands. Some are good in FMCG area and some are good in Automobiles. Look for proven success in your own area.

c) Every agency has a few stars and many followers. Make sure the stars are in the agency and have not shifted to any other agency. Choose an agency where you are sure the best of the agency will work on your account. A market tour of clients and Brand managers will give you information on it.

d) **Agencies have flavors. There are creativity driven agencies and research driven agencies. Examine your need and decide.**

e) Create an evaluation system involving strategy, creative, media planning, return on campaign, domain success and so on and give proper weightage to each element to compare different agencies. It is a one-time detailed exercise but serves the company for long, every time you have to select an advertising agency

63) **How to work with an Advertising agency?**
Brand Managers work with advertising agencies in two different modes; a) Client is always right where they do what they wish and the agency allows it to happen as it keeps the account safe with them b) The agency professionals dominate the company Brand managers since they (Brand Managers) don't have adequate knowledge especially in the area of Aesthetics.

Some suggestions to engage productively with the advertising agency are given here,

a) Get adequate knowledge in Brand aesthetics so you can articulate why something is good or not good in

terms of color, form, typography and composition

b) Never be overwhelmed by the agency professionals. If they show you the portfolio of the agency be clear is it not just the work of people you are dealing with, rather it is the work of many over many years

c) Subject to consumer testing everything that is being considered or is to be released

d) **Always have campaign returns study done to ascertain the good and not good work of the agency. Never interfere where you don't understand, don't spoil the good work of the advertising agency.**

e) Lastly always remember it is the 'one great idea' which makes or breaks a campaign the rest is 'execution'. Ensure you insist on a 'great idea' and never approve a campaign without it. Always have in mind the all-time great campaigns like 'Fevicol' and 'Sony' for inspiration.

64) Which are some of the world's best advertisements ever made?

In the history of advertising some of the best advertisements ever made are a must see for any person interested in the area. Given below is a list of television advertisements which are all-time greats. Similar quality advertisements of press, hoardings you should see. Do also see all-time great work in public relations and event management. Each of the advertisements given below is 'great' in a different sense. They are also from varied time periods and varied country contexts.

a) Honda, The Cog
   https://www.youtube.com/watch?v=_ve4M4UsJQo
b) **Sony Bouncing Balls**
   https://www.youtube.com/watch?v=7DrFY3H-u8w
c) Sony Bouncing Rabbits
   https://www.youtube.com/watch?v=CLUAbkRUvVQ
d) **Isuzu Dancing in Paris**
   https://www.youtube.com/watch?v=T-VEMVAB1hc
e) Thai life insurance
   https://www.youtube.com/watch?v=K9vFWA1rnWc
f) **Liril**
   https://www.youtube.com/watch?v=Gm2XNb6-iOM
g) Government of India
   https://www.youtube.com/watch?v=-jf6pwtPqCs
h) **Fevicol, Bus Top**

https://www.youtube.com/wa tch?v=jURZhtMX914

i) Volvo Lifepaint
https://www.youtube.com/wa tch?v=CfWzeGlaFvI&index=1&li st=PLUqM01q0yFwwFi04LCvVB FrNrTFLkehvM

j) Lijjat Papad
https://www.youtube.com/wa tch?v=24mbYBH95H4&list=PLh gnBue3FjS1UaszaMj5FPFLsG7rv L0Bn&index=6

65) What is Corporate Identity?

Corporate Identity refers to the collection of visual elements that come together to create a visual identity for the corporate. The corporate identity is created by the visual look, feel and experience of the company name, logo, letter head, visiting cards, packaging, transport graphics, retail graphics and so on. The corporate identity creates in the mind of the audience an image of the corporate and hence a response to that image which may be positive or negative.

66) **What is the Corporate Identity Manual?**

Corporate Identity Manual is a document created by the advertising agency which gives **specifics** in terms of color code (pantone number), fonts used, size of fonts, the exact distance of every visual element from the (paper or print material) boundaries and so on. This document is essentially used for Printing or Production.

The company gives a copy of this document to retailers to ensure the boards they put up on their shops, the glow-signs, the in-store communication and so on is consistent across all shops. On the lines of the Corporate Identity Manual one can also create a Brand

Identity Manual for use by the advertising agency, company, retailers and event managers engaged in the Brand campaign.

67) **What is a Campaign Returns Study?**

Companies essentially work on the principle of RoI (Return on Investment). The company RoI naturally depends on the RoI of all the four functional areas viz. Marketing, Operations, Finance and Human Resources. In the consumer marketing space the RoI of Marketing is the most important contributor to the Corporate RoI. Hence RoI of the Marketing function gains significance. In turn the RoI of the marketing area is heavily dependent on the RoI of Brand Management (a sub function of marketing). Hence today in the consumer marketing space, the RoI on Brand spend determines the RoI of

Marketing and that in turn determines the RoI of the corporate.

It is necessary hence to ascertain the RoI of Brand Management area and for that it is necessary to ascertain the Returns on Campaign since that is a major part of Brand spend.

Campaign Returns Study provides us with the RoI of the campaign including both short term returns and the long term returns. Campaign Returns Study should preferably be done by an independent third party who doesn't have any involved conflict of interest.

68) **How to do a campaign returns study?**
Campaign returns study can be done using many approaches. One approach is to use the consumer's brand adoption process. Here we measure before and after the campaign parameters viz.; a)

Brand awareness b) Brand comprehension c) Brand preference d) Brand Usage e) Brand loyalty

On the basis of gain or loss in these parameters the return on campaign is arrived at and the same is then read in the light of Brand equity.

A house of brands is like a family, each needs a role and a relationship to others
Jeffrey Sinclair

MAINTAINING THE BRAND

A Brand is a living entity - and it is enriched or undermined cumulatively over time, the product of a thousand small gestures

Michael Eisner, CEO Disney

69) What is Brand maintenance?

Inorder to maintain the Brand in face of competition, companies deploy a variety of Brand measures. Some of these measures are everyday measures called tactical measures and some of these are long term measures called Strategic measures. Brand maintenance means deploying strategic and tactical measures to keep the Brand strong in the market in the face of competition.

70) What are the strategic measures deployed by the company for Brand maintenance?

The Strategic measures deployed by the company for Brand maintenance are,

      a)   Brand Extension

      b)   Brand Repositioning

      c)   Brand Relaunching

71) What is Brand Extension?

Brand Extension refers to stretching a Brand to sell more than one product under the name of the brand. There are two schools in Brand Management with respect to the phenomenon of Brand extension. One school led by Jack Trout believes that Brand extension in the long run dilutes Brand equity and so should never be done whereas the other school led by David Aaker and Kepferer believe in Brand extension (ofcourse done in a judicious way) since they believe it leads unlocking the latent equity and brings down the cost, time and risk associated with a new Brand launch.

Brand Extension can be of varied types, it can be the Corporate Brand extended to cover many product categories or it can be a product category Brand extended to cover many products or it can be a collective Brand used by many companies operating in a given area or it can be like in case of GE where a corporate Brand is extended to support the product category Brand (Opel) which inturn is extended to support another Brand (Astra).

Brand extension has been deeply researched and studied. Brand Failures that have occurred due to extension have been extensively analyzed. Guidelines for Brand extensions have now been arrived at from experience. One rule of thumb is, where the

purchase decision is guided by psychological factors and the product is a simple product, focused brand works better and where the product is of high cost or high technical complexity and the purchase decision is not guided primarily by psychological preferences, there Brand extension especially of the corporate Brand works well.

Dettol had a restricted sale owing to it being a product for occasional use. Dettol as a Brand then was used only when one was injured. To find new occasions for the Brand use, a Brand extension was thought of and 'Dettol Soap' was launched. The Soap had an everyday use compared to the erstwhile disinfectant. This has been one of the best examples of Brand extension where the extension has unlocked the latent value of the brand.

Rolls Royce has kept its sharp focused architecture and has never given into extending the Brand to other automobile product. Although extension would lead to short term benefits, it would erode Brand equity in the long run.

One of the difficulties in today's era of short duration employee stays in the organization has been of Brand Managers recklessly extending brands to show revenue growth, taking bonuses and fleeing, leaving the Brand weakened in the long run.

72) **What is Brand Repositioning?**

Brand positioning is a long term decision. Every company wants the Brand once positioned to be there for atleast 5-10 years. However certain events in the market place or within the company can lead the company to rethink on the present positioning of a given Brand. The company may decide hence to change the 'positioning' of the Brand. This action is referred to as 'Brand repositioning'.

Brand repositioning is a high cost, high risk and high time consuming activity. Some reasons that force the company to consider Brand repositioning are given here,

a) Customer profiles are changing and the Brand has to radically change to continue being relevant to the customer e.g. Grasim

b) **The Brand has to appeal to a new segment of customers who are radically different from the present customers e.g. Suzuki Nexa**

c) The Brand is to be extended to cover new products and appeal to new customers e.g. Dettol

d) Competition has repositioned its Brands and our Brand continues to be as it was years before and now looks out of date and boring e.g. Zandu

e) Owing to inefficient everyday Brand management, Brand Alteration required over time was done and its cumulative result is a wide gap now between the customer and the Brand and there is no way except repositioning to bridge that gap e.g. Vimal

Brand repositioning in practice has been a bag of successes and failures, some companies have succeeded in repositioning and some have failed. If a Brand repositioning fails, it is a costly blow to the company. The company has to think of a 're-repositioning' which is an even more risky and costly imperative.

73) What is Brand Re-launching?

Brands fail in the market owing to 'Brand reasons' and owing to 'non-brand reasons'. A Brand like 'Yardley' can fail (in certain markets) owing to 'Brand reasons' while a Brand like 'Nokia' can fail owing to non-Brand reasons. Nokia as a Brand failed because of 'not going along' with android (failure due to product features) and not because it's advertising or public relations was not good enough.

If the Brand has failed owing to non-Brand reasons then the Brand often enjoys preference in the minds of customers which can be harvested by re-launching the Brand with changes made with respect to the 'non-brand reasons' which led to failure in the first place.

Brand re-launching hence is an action where an erstwhile Brand which still enjoys preference in the minds of the customers is re-launched. The re-launch is generally done to address the same product segment as before. In developing countries like India there are many erstwhile Brands which have failed in the last twenty years owing to non-Brand reasons and yet they enjoy immense latent equity in the minds of customers and there is a huge portfolio of such assets waiting to be actualized.

Take an example. Nokia as a Brand still enjoys liking and preference in people's minds even though the Brand has failed. If this Brand was to be re-launched with right changes made to product features and price, the Brand stands to enjoy a bright future. There is a strong case for 're-launching' of 'Nokia'.

The cost, risk and time involved in re-launching has to be weighed against a new Brand creation or a potential Brand extension before a Brand re-launching decision is taken. Often in many situations there is no Brand available for a re-launching and hence there the possibility doesn't exist.

74) **What are the Brand Tactics deployed by companies in the course of everyday Brand Management?**

Companies usually deploy three tactical measures towards everyday Brand Management. The three measures are,

   a)   Brand Alteration
   b)   **Brand Rejuvenation**
   c)   Co-branding

75) **What is Brand Alteration?**

Brand Alteration refers to the small changes that are intentionally brought about or that happen unintentionally in the mind of the audience over a period of time, with regard to Brand associations, Brand image or Brand personality. With every campaign a few associations are added, deleted or modified, knowingly or unknowingly.

The Brand is a dynamic entity and it is never static. Owing to communication, product experience, intra psychic processing in the mind of the audience and action by competition, Brand alteration keeps happening over time.

Companies use Brand Alteration to fight competition and overcome monotony in Brand communication. Often owing to changes happening in the Customer Profile, Brand Alteration becomes a necessity. If not done on right time, the gap between what the Brand stands for and what the customer wants increases and when this gap becomes too large to be handled by Alteration then Brand

Repositioning becomes an imperative. Brand Alteration not done on time accumulates over time leading to an imperative of Brand repositioning which is far more costly and risk involving.

76) **What is Brand Rejuvenation?**

Over a period of time campaigns cease to create the WoW effect and they are forgotten in the clutter of competing campaigns. Brands become boring and monotonous. In such a situation to distinctly stand out from the clutter and provide a WoW effect, Companies often deploy a Brand Rejuvenation (some call it Revitalization) campaign.

Such a campaign is distinct in terms of a theme, flavor, large budget and (often) use of celebrity endorsement. Often such campaigns are also accompanied by special edition product launches and promotional offers. Such campaigns make the Brand vivid in the mind-space of the customer. During Brand rejuvenation campaigns, the Brand can temporarily enjoy the 'top of the mind recall' status. An occasional Brand Rejuvenation campaign is good for every brand. E.g. Scooty Pink campaign.

77) What is Co-Branding?

Co-branding refers to two Brands jointly doing a campaign often involving a joint sale of both products. Co-branding arrangements are extremely difficult to arrive at since it is not easy to ascertain who gains how much from it and correspondingly how much should each pay for it.

It is also difficult to ascertain how long could the 'Co-Journey' go on. Most Co-Branding campaigns are short term campaigns, mostly accompanied by joint sale of products. Needless to say such arrangements are mostly possible only between non-competing companies having complimenting products.

A Brand for a company is like a reputation for a person. You earn reputation by trying to do hard things well.
Jeff Bezos

EVALUATING BRAND EQUITY

A Brand is not a product or a promise or a feeling. It's the sum of all the experiences you have with a company
Amir Kassaei, Chief Creative Officer, DDB Global

78) What is Brand Equity?

Brand Equity refers to the monetary worth of the brand. In simple words Brand equity of a Brand means if you were to sell the Brand today what amount would you get for the brand.

79) What are the four essential approaches to evaluate Brand Equity?

Brand Equity deals with two aspects, the present profits from the Brand and the future profits from the Brand. It is the future profits which are difficult to measure and so a variety of (indirect) models are used to measure it.

There are many models to measure Brand Equity and all those models can be classified into four groups viz.,

a)   Sales based Models
b)   Premium based Models
c)   Market Capitalization Models
d)   Customer centric Models

The Sales based Models try to predict the future sales of the Brand and from there arrive at the present worth of the Brand or Brand Equity. The Premium based Models look not at sales but at the 'margin' that the Brand enjoys. Naturally that part of the 'margin' which is owing to product quality, availability, service and so on has to be deducted from this 'margin' if one has to sell only the Brand and not the production and distribution entities. This method is good if one has to look at the 'value add' by the Advertising agency. Based on the 'margins', Brand equity is arrived at. The Market Capitalization Models look at the total market capitalization of the company as being the sum total of market capitalization of all the Brands of the company. From this corpus each Brand is apportioned its Brand Equity value.

The Customer centric models take into account the objective and psychological aspects involved in Brand purchase and ascertain Brand Equity from there. Issues like Brand awareness, Brand comprehension, and Brand preference are taken into account apart from present sales in this approach.

Every approach and model has its own strength, weakness and therefore a context for application.

80) What are some of the popular Brand Equity measurement models?

Some of the popular Brand Equity measurement Models are,

1. **Young and Rubicam's Brand Asset Evaluator**
2. **Millward Brown's Brand Dynamics Pyramid and Brandz Map**
3. **Interbrand's Brand Equity Model**
4. **Financial world's Brand Equity Model**
5. **Houlihan's Brand Equity Model**
6. **BBDO's Brand Equity Model**
7. **A C Nielson's Brand Equity Model**
8. **Epsos's Brand Equity Model**
9. **Research International's Brand Equity Model**
10. **SDR Consulting's Brand Equity Model**
11. **M/A/R/C's Brand Equity Model**

12. Brand Finance Plc's Brand Equity Model
13. Keller's Brand Equity Model
14. Aaker's Brand Equity Model

81) How to select a Brand equity measurement model?

The right Brand equity model can be selected based on the context and in the light of some of the criteria given here,

a) Objective of the Brand equity evaluation

b) Strength and weakness of available methods

c) Legal aspects involved in the context

d) Difficulty of using a model in a given context

e) Time and Cost involved in using any given method

82) **Can multiple Brand equity models be used for evaluating Brand equity?**
Yes it is possible. Each method based upon its nature and assumptions used will give a different figure of Brand equity. Hence based on the requirement in the given context either one of more of the Brand equity methods can be used by the company.

For example which evaluating worth of the Brand for a public issue the company may use the market capitalization method while the same company for evaluating the work of its advertising agency may use the premium method.

83) **What are the aspects related to Brand Equity that the company has to engage with?**

There are three main aspects related to Brand Equity that every company has to engage with. The three aspects are,

a) **Measurement of Brand Equity**

On a regular basis with a consistently followed method, Brand Equity has to be measured to ensure the capital formation aspect of brand-spend is rightly reflected in the balance sheet and is recognized as a property and a strategic asset created for the company.

b) **Enhancement of Brand Equity**

Return on Campaign Studies have to be linked with the Brand Equity measurement efforts to clarify how each campaign has affected and added to the existing Brand Equity.

c) **Leveraging**

   Brand Equity is a form of property and a strategic asset and it has to be leveraged for raising resources or in merger and acquisition processes.

84) **What is a Brand Management system?**

   Brand Management system is a conceptual system backed by required IT infrastructure and an information system to manage the Brands of the company on a long term basis. The Brand management system deals with issues of Brand strategy, Creatives, Media planning, Brand portfolio, Brand profitability, return on Brand spend and so on. The system also serves as an archive enabling use of past data and finding insights by processing past data. It also serves as a resource library for Brand management.

The system also houses research and findings on a long term basis providing a rich matrix for data mining. Brand management system is found instituted partly or completely only in companies which are 'mature' in the context of 'Brand Management'.

85) **Are there softwares available to help the Brand Management system?**

Yes there are a variety of softwares available to help in the area of Brand management. Some softwares focus on Brand equity while some others focus on the creative aspects. Most softwares have an area of focus while some softwares cover the entire area of Brand Management. Some subscription services are also available especially in the area of media planning.

Some of the popular softwares available are given here,

a) Brand folder

b) Marcom Central Enterprise

c) Brand Centre

d) Honeycomb Archive

e) PubliSphere

f) Branding Manager

g) BEMapps

h) Campaign Drive

i) MarCom On Demand

j) Market Smart 360

k) Media Vault

l) Watch My Competitor

You can't build a reputation on what you are
going to do
Henry Ford

COMPANY CULTURE AND BRAND MANAGEMENT

It takes 20 years to build a reputation and five minutes to ruin it. If you think about that, you'll do things differently

Warren Buffet

86) What is Company Culture?

Every company has written and unwritten norms that people consciously or unconsciously follow. Culture consists of these norms which include values, attitudes, orientation and convention. The company culture can have a flavor of being autocratic, democratic, either creative or numbers driven and so on.

87) What is a Brand Culture?

Every company has a culture. Brand culture refers to what place the 'Brand culture' has in the company's culture. It is a subset of the company culture.

In some companies 'Brand Management' is supposed to be an activity of the 'Brand Management Team' and people in other departments don't realize nor are they told what impact their actions of omission or commission have on the 'Brand' in the market and how that in turn that affects the company profits and their own well-being.

While in other companies everyone knows what 'Brands' the company owns, what these Brands stand for in the market and how they are strengthened or weakened owing to an action or inaction by a company employee. Such a company is credited with having created a 'Good Brand Culture'.

The Brand Culture of a company thus lies on a continuum of a Good Brand Culture to an absence of Brand Culture.

88) **What are the four types of Brand Cultures that prevail in organizations?**

Brand Culture within a company can qualitatively range from a Good Brand Culture to an absence of a Brand Culture. The four types of 'Brand Cultures' that exist in organizations are,

   a. **Primitive Brand Management Culture**
   b. Creativity led Brand Management Culture
   c. **Research led Brand Management Culture**
   d. Strategic Brand Management Culture

89) What are the features of the Brand culture referred to as 'Primitive Brand Management Culture'?

The primitive Brand Culture is said to exist when the company hardly knows enough about what do in the area of 'Brand Management'. The efforts of the company are not systematic and happen in an OFF and ON mode. There is no campaign thinking nor is any Advertising agency given a brief to create one. There is no deep consumer research nor a clarity on deployment of aesthetics. Small and Medium enterprises or Non-Profit organizations when they start deploying Brand Management often start with this Brand Culture.

90) What are the features of the Brand culture referred to as 'Creativity led Brand Management Culture'?

In Creativity led Brand Management Culture, the company is clear about the concept of a Brand Campaign and there is a synergy and congruence between varied creative tools used. The company observes the identity manual at the corporate and the Brand levels. The creative ideas on which the campaigns are based are not yet derived from customer research but are intuitively arrived at. Brand Management Culture that has appreciated the need for a systematic process to Brand Management but falls short of incorporating research in the process in a major way is termed as Creativity led Brand Management Culture.

91) **What are the features of the Brand culture referred to as 'Research led Brand Management Culture'?**

As the Brand Culture in the company matures, Research is intensively used in the process of Brand Management. Research is used in areas of Brand strategy, Architecture, Positioning, Creative, Consumer testing and so on. Most important is the Campaign Returns Study which is an anchor research study across campaigns. Such a Brand culture in the company is referred to as a research led Brand management culture.

92) What are the features of the Brand culture referred to as 'Strategic Brand Management Culture'?

The maturity of the Brand Culture is the highest when it reaches the state of 'Strategic Brand Culture'. In this state the company looks at Brand Management as a Strategic activity and top Management is involved in every critical Brand activity. The company also looks now at Brand Equity as a form of property and gets into its regular monitoring and leveraging for strategic purposes. The company in Management of its Brand portfolio and product portfolio moves from Brand portfolio to the product portfolio and not the other way around. New products are developed to fill defined Brand gaps rather than new brands being developed to sell products made from identification of product gaps in the product portfolio. The Brand culture at this stage has to span pan-organization and regardless of function or level, the basics related to the Brands the company has in the market, are known by everyone. Such a Brand culture is referred to as a strategic Brand management culture.

93) How do you create a good Brand Culture in the Organization?

Creating a 'Brand Culture' in any organization needs sustained efforts. Sustained in-company communication is the center piece of action. Further everyone in the company has to know what bearing his actions or his department's actions is on the Company Brands. The rational and psychological factors going into Brand creation has to be communicated and when a mistake is committed it has to be explained in the context of the Brand damage and overall customer dissatisfaction it can cause bearing upon company profits and then on to the employees. Adequate reward systems based on good work contributing to Brand management, also has to be instituted in the company. Creating a 'Brand Culture' also needs a long term orientation, ethical working and nurturing creativity in the organization. Lastly it is the top management involvement and the significance they accord to Brand Management in words, actions and policies is what truly communicates and institutes a good Brand culture in the company.

94) **What are the examples in practice of each of the above stated Brand Cultures?**

Some examples of each 'type' of Brand cultures above stated are given here,

Company	Type of Brand Culture
Johnson and Johnson	Strategic
P&G	Strategic
Tata	Research
Suzuki	Research
Bajaj	Creativity
Himalaya	Creativity
Patanjali	Primitive

Brands are arguably the key assets that a company possesses and they should therefore be a top-priority for senior management and not seen as something left solely to the marketing department. They represent the embodiment of a company's differentiation and positioning.

Chris Halliburton, professor of international marketing, ESCP Europe

PART III

BRAND MANAGEMENT:
SPECIALITY AREAS

When people use your Brand name as a verb,
that is remarkable
Meg Whitman

Chinese consumers are brand-loyal because
they are reluctant to try something new, not
because they actively love the incumbents
Ratan Malli, Director, JWT Shanghai

CULT BRANDS

If people believe they share values with a company, they will stay loyal to the brand
Howard Schultz, Starbucks

95) What is a Cult Brand?
Cult Brands are the brands that are used by a group of customers who are a small distinct group in the society. The group is distinct by virtue of appearance, belief or a way of life. The Cult Brand is generally used by this group to make a statement of being offbeat. Often this 'statement' has an undertone of iconoclasm or defiance built into it.

Harley Davidson is a good example of a Cult Brand.

96) Why do groups of customer's patronize the Cult Brands?

Cults are groups which wish to express their distinctiveness in the face of the mainstream. This often is a result of their (cult group members) hidden feelings of inferiority, rage or in some cases a radical disagreement on an issue of belief. Members of such groups wish to publicly express their inner feelings and preferences and stand out as distinct from the mainstream society. Self-expression by public use of products is one mode of making a statement. Such are the reasons for customers to patronize a Cult Brand.

97) How do you create a Cult Brand?

Creating a Cult Brand is not easy and is a high risk endeavor with often limited returns. One has to first identify a Cult with adequate purchasing power. One has to then identify the products the

Cult would like to invest in and if these product making is our area of strength. One has to be innovative enough, for no Cult is going to patronize an ordinary product or a product which doesn't innovate enough to help the Cult speak the 'Cult Statement'. The product, communication and the retail experience then has to be made congruent to the Cult preferences. Public Relations and Events have a very strong role to play here. Mass media is leveraged initially to a high intensity and then dropped down to keep within the confines of the budget. It is not easy to find a celebrity to do endorsement for Cult Brands for the celebrity in real life has to have a real life persona that fits the Cult Brand. Across the Brand Management and product development process, one has to be in intimate contact with the Cult to understand their minds and address the deep unsaid desires.

98) Can the Cult Brand ever become a mass brand?

Yes it can happen. Apple is the best example of it. In its difficult times, Apple was a Cult Brand and after iPhone it has become a mass brand.

99) Are Cult Brands financially viable?

Yes and No. It all depends on the size, concentration and purchasing power of the Cult. A Cult spread too thin across the world is no good, so is a Cult which is present only in one country and in too small a number or a Cult with very low purchasing power. Such Cults won't be able to make a Cult Brand financially viable however if one finds the right size, concentration and adequate purchasing power with a Cult then it becomes a financially viable proposition to create a Cult Brand.

100) Can Cult brands be extended?

Yes and No. It is an extremely contextual question and the answer is based on; a) which Cult are we addressing b) by which product are we addressing the Cult c) What values does the Brand stand for now and d) to which product is it going to be extended.

A Harley Davidson can be extended to tough and off beat off-roaders but not to shaving creams or baby products.

101) Can Cult brands ever aspire to grow into a multi-billion dollar league?

Yes and No. It depends on the purchasing power of the Cult you are addressing, their spending on your product, margins and the global size of the Cult. If you create a Cult Car in the Rolls Royce category then yes you can enter the multi-billion dollar league. If like Harley Davidson you can have a Cult in 25 countries than too the answer is yes. However if the Cult is too small and present in only one or two countries then you can't get into the multi-billion dollar league.

102) **Can Cult Brands be associated to a religion or a philosophical belief?**

In theory yes. Groups based on shared religious or philosophical beliefs could have been the constituencies of a Cult Brand. However ironically, all existing Cult Brands are secular in nature. Yet the fact remains that philosophical or religious beliefs can be addressed by Cult Brands if the said beliefs are shared by a small group and if the beliefs are radically different from those shared by the mainstream society. Some of the issues have been the size and purchasing power of such groups, their stability and the opinion of its leader. Hopefully on the front of philosophical beliefs in times to come we will see development of some Cult Brands. On the whole the power of Cult Brands stands under leveraged in the area of Brand Management.

103) Is communication or the product more important in case of Cult Brands?

Both the product and the communication have to be off-beat. It has to be different from the mainstream and has to address the needs of the Cult Group. It has to make the Cult members feel distinct, often superior, iconoclastic or defiant. Of the two, communication is more important than the product for even if other mainstream brands copy the product they can never copy the Brand image.

104) **Is it possible to create Cult brands in developing or under-developed countries?**

It is difficult but not impossible. In developing societies it is not easy to be iconoclastic or defiant and assert once distinctness in contrast to the mainstream society. Also the amount of money such Cult Groups can spend on the Cult Brand is very limited and so often the financial viability doesn't support creation of a Cult Brand. Vegans and the Organic Cult groups however have been able to create strong constituencies and financially viable Cult Brands have come up and are doing well. On the other hand, there have been attempts by feminists and homosexual groups to create Cult brands. The effort as yet has not been successful.

INGREDIENT BRANDING

105) What is Ingredient branding?

Every product that we consume is made up of 'ingredients'. If you consume a biscuit, it is made up of flour, sugar, additives, preservatives and so on. We know the 'brand' and 'producer' of the final product 'the biscuit' however we don't have any knowledge about the 'brand' or 'producer' of any of the ingredients of the final product we use. Most Ingredient producers are small and medium enterprises except some of them like automobile vendors which are companies of a large size.

Ingredient branding refers to the phenomenon of leveraging Brand Management to create and manage a Brand for an 'Ingredient'.

Ingredients are of two types viz.; a) Ingredients which are components that is they can be distinctly seen in the final product, say compressor (an ingredient) of a refrigerator and b) Ingredients which enter into a self-changing process in the process of product creation and so can no longer be seen as they were added, say the sugar added to the biscuit can no longer be separately seen in the biscuit. Ingredient Branding can be deployed for both these types of Ingredients.

106) Is it possible to create a B2B Ingredient Brand?

Yes it is possible to create a B2B Ingredient Brand or a B2C Ingredient brand, both are possible.

107) What is the significance of ingredient branding?

For every product available as a Brand in the market there are atleast 10-25 Ingredient producers behind the product without whom the product could not have been made. However the customer doesn't know the ingredient producers and so they are ill-treated by the Brand owner as a 'commodity supplier' to be squeezed and exploited. The margins of ingredient producers are very low. The Ingredient producer is also dispensable since he has no touch with the final customer.

One way to overcome this situation is for the Ingredient producer to create an 'Ingredient brand'. Intel is the best example of Ingredient branding. Today this ingredient Brand is far stronger than the final brands of which it is a part. Customers don't buy many final brands if they don't have this ingredient Brand as their chief Ingredient.

108) Can any ingredient producer create an ingredient brand?

In an essential sense, one creates a Brand only if it is profitable to do so. The same principle applies here. If the Ingredient producer has the prospect of adequate gain in terms of sales and margins to justify the creation of a Brand then the producer goes for it.

The best Ingredients for which an Ingredient Brand can be created are Ingredients which are of high value and critical to the functioning of the final product. Take compressor in a refrigerator or microprocessor in a computer or engine in an automobile. Some Ingredients which are not so high cost may be critical in terms of health or safety, take for example 'low sodium salt' used in food industry or at home or the main switch fuse used to protect the house or office from power fluctuations.

Such Ingredients are also good candidates to create an Ingredient brand.

In theory for any Ingredient an Ingredient Brand can be created. Take a real example. In USA one of the 'screw' producers used to produce screws used in fixing the wooden roofs to the wooden columns. The cost of the screw was very low and so were the margins. During storms it was these screws that used to break and allow the roof to be damaged or flown away. A Brand campaign was created on this criticality of the 'screw' which led to either safety or to economic hazards. 'Don't screw with the screw', 'It is the screw of Safety' and so on the communication went on to say. The Ingredient Brand was created. Customers started asking for this particular screw to be used in construction. The sales and margins of the producer went up dramatically. If a screw can be branded so can anything else be from salt to space shuttle ingredients.

109) Is it financially viable to create an ingredient brand?

If the potential market size and margins are adequate then yes. The Ingredient Brand grows like any other Brand partly by appropriating market share of other Brands and partly by market size growth.

The question of viability is more relevant when one is talking about a B2C brand. In case the Ingredient is used in making an Industrial product, the Ingredient Brand creation becomes a B2B Brand creation which does not involve mass media in a major way and so is affordable involving low risk.

However if the Ingredient Branding involves a B2C Brand creation then financial viability may be a critical question since mass media is involved in the effort and Brand spend is considerable.

110) **What are the direct and indirect benefits of ingredient branding?**

Direct benefits include; a) Higher sales b) Higher margins c) Reduction in 'dispensability' at the hands of the producer of the final Brand d) Customer loyalty

Indirect benefits include; a) Higher market capitalization b) Consideration (positive) in tendering processes c) Ease in raising financial resources for growth d) Ability to use the Ingredient Brand as a Strategic currency especially in the Merger and Acquisitions process

111) **Which are the sectors where there is a great potential for creating an Ingredient Brand?**

It is question that has a different answer across countries and markets. However some of the most common and promising candidates to create an Ingredient Brand the world over are,

a) **Compressors used in Refrigerators**

b) Microprocessors used for computing in computer or mobile

c) **Engine or Clutch used in automobiles**

d) Chemicals used in food industry

e) **Plastic insulation used in electrical industry**

f) Adhesives used in varied applications

g) **Material used for Construction and Interior Décor**

112) Can Venture Capital, Private Equity other resource avenues help the process of Ingredient Branding?

Absolutely yes. If an Ingredient producer with long standing experience and quality record is available, investors can invest as a portfolio investor and then divest post establishment of the Brand reaping a profitable harvest. Alternately, the Ingredient producer can offer an equity stake –in lieu of cash- to advertising agencies and media houses to create the Ingredient brand.

113) Can celebrity endorsement help in ingredient branding?

Yes Indeed. The use of a celebrity overnight builds familiarity, trust and liking for the brand. Especially if the celebrity has values associated with himself which can be of value to the Ingredient Brand it leads to a higher value add to the brand. Smaller

Ingredient producers can't afford a celebrity however larger ones can. Smaller Ingredient producers often give a small share of equity to the celebrity for endorsing the brand.

114) Can a collective Brand like a geographical indicator be leveraged for ingredient branding?

Yes it can be. Some collective brands like 'Basmati' (for rice) and 'Swiss' (for watch movements) are being used by Ingredient producers to sell their producer to the final product maker.

The collective Brand model is an area where Governments and multilateral donor agencies can help (by part financing) to create a common Ingredient Brand which can then be used (under license) by a number of small and medium size producers.

INDUSTRIAL BRANDS

115) What are Industrial Brands?

Industrial products are products which are sold by one company to another. The buyer of the product uses the product for the purpose of manufacturing some other product and not self-consumption. It is a B2B (business to business) sale and not a B2C (Business to Consumer) sale. Brands under which Industrial products are sold are called Industrial brands.

Examples of Industrial products are, steering for cars, compressors for air conditioners, circuit boards for computers, Oil and grease used in manufacturing, chemicals used in manufacturing or preservatives for food products. Brands under which these products are sold are called Industrial Brands.

116) Are all Industrial Brands essentially Ingredient brands?

Not always. There are industrial products like Capital Goods, Lubricants of machines, Power supply products which are used for the production process which become ingredients of the final products. Such products are Industrial products but not Ingredients. Thus all ingredient products are industrial products but all industrial products are not ingredients.

To add to the complexity some ingredient brands are created targeting the final customer and hence they are B2C brands rather than B2B brands. Thus all ingredient brands are not necessarily industrial brands rather some of them are consumer brands. Thus we have possibilities viz. Ingredient products sold under an industrial brand (Bilt Papers), ingredient products sold under consumer brands (Intel), industrial product sold under an Industrial Brand (Fanuc, Mirac CNC machines) and Industrial product sold under a customer brand (SAP software). Industrial products being sold under a customer brand is not an accurate and complete description of practice, infact in this situation the Brand is managed partly as an Industrial Brand and partly as a Customer Brand.

117) What is the difference between creating a consumer Brand and an Industrial brand?

Consumer marketing always deals with millions of anonymous customers (or potential customers) which is not the case in Industrial marketing. Purchase decision in case of Industrial products is made primarily on the basis of price, quality, time for delivery and after sales service. Since it is essentially a rational decision making process involving technical knowledge and testing, subjective psychological value addition has its limitations. Industrial Brand Management doesn't need mass media since target audience most of the times is 'industrial customers' and not final customers in the society. Industrial Brand Management hence uses very less of mass media since society in general is not the target audience and the campaign uses more of events, focused technical communication to clients (and potential clients) supported with a small amount of public relations effort.

118) Do Industrial Brands occasionally release communication to address the lay customer?

Yes they do. Take for instance Tata Steel has long standing Brand campaign titled 'We also make Steel' and its competitor SAIL too has a long standing Band campaign 'There is a bit of SAIL in everyone's life'. Both these Industrial Brands are also targeting lay audience with their Brand campaign. Similar is the story with Intel and AMD.

Such B2C campaigns can have multiple objectives viz.; a) creating a loyalty base amongst final customers b) to prepare ground before launching the public offer on the stock exchange c) Create a psychological preference to influence the tender or bulk purchase process.

119) Do Industrial brands use public relations as tool more than any other communication vehicle while addressing the general citizens?

No. Generally Industrial Brands prefer focused technical communication and event participation for Branding. However at times a few industrial brands do use public relations as the primary vehicle to create a Brand with regard to final customers. Often such brands are the ones that wish to; a) participate in government tenders or large EPC contracts or b) create a good image on front of environment, human rights and corporate governance or c) Create a positive context for an upcoming public issue or d) Create a positive context before undertaking a large scale strategic event that can alter the competitive landscape.

BRAND MANAGEMENT FOR SMALL AND MEDIUM ENTERPRISES

120) What is low cost Brand Management?

With mass media costs going very high, small and medium companies are searching for ways to practice low cost Brand Management. It is easier to do it in the area of Industrial Brands than in case of consumer brands since industrial branding doesn't make much use of mass media.

Low cost Brand Management also means celebrity endorsement is no longer an option and 'action per week' in terms of campaign elements is also goes on the lower side. Digital marketing has opened up new possibilities for low cost Brand Management by efficient targeting and a very low cost per contact. Low cost Brand Management hence comes to mean a public relations and event's heavy Brand Campaign with use of targeted and digital communication.

121) Can small and medium enterprises leverage low cost Brand Management?

Yes they can. Infact they leverage digital marketing, communication in trade or technical magazines and events to build the brand. Leveraging collective brands is also a powerful method that can be used by small and medium industries provided all players involved can work together in harmony which is not easy but possible.

122) What is phased development of the Brand territory?

If funds are a problem or if distribution or after sales service systems across the country are not ready, one can have a phased launch of a brand. It means you launch the Brand first in a state then in a few more states and then take it nation-wide. Once established in the country you can take it pan continent and then to another continent and then global. Over a period of 10 years a global Brand can be established. If such is the Brand roll out plan then you focus your Brand campaign based on your territory. You use newspaper editions, magazines, radio channels specific to that territory. This is called phased development of Brand territory where you gradually expand the territory where the Brand is available and hence where the Brand campaign is active. If the Brand territory is a State then print media is more cost effective and if the Brand territory is national then television is more cost effective.

123) How do small and medium enterprises hire an Advertising agency and work with it?

The small and medium scale companies can't afford any of the top ten advertising agencies. The best way to work for them is to hire an individual Brand consultant and a small advertising agency with good creative ability. The Brand consultant provides the strategy, research and the quality control part while creative and operations are taken care of by the small advertising agency. Many such agencies manned by designers or artists exist in the market that are good in creative but not so good in strategy or research.

124) **Have there been examples of small and medium enterprises leveraging Brand Management to graduate to a large company?**

Yes there are many examples. In India Brands like Nirma, Ramdev, Parachute were once small and medium enterprises which today are large companies. Much of their success was owing to successful leveraging of Brand Management. With long term investment horizon they have successfully come up with strong brands and have graduated to a large scale.

BRAND MANAGEMENT FOR NON-PROFITS

125) Can Non-Profits deploy and benefit from Brand Management?

Yes they can. Infact many of the most successful Non-Profit organizations have deployed Brand Management to great benefit for their beneficiaries, their causes and their organizations.

126) What are the areas where non-profits can use Brand Management?

Non-Profits can use Brand Management in areas viz.; a) In social communication and advocacy projects inorder to inform people, change their attitude or approach in areas of gender justice, child rights, animal rights, de-addiction and so on. B) In selling products made by poor beneficiaries in the world market or local market by creating a Brand for these products c) Create a collective Brand for a number of small producers who can all use the Brand d) To create a Brand for their organization to raise funds and get volunteers e) Help small producers use Brand Management to the extent they can by leveraging low cost Brand Management

127) **Does a low cost model exist for non-profits to use the knowledge of Brand Management for a social cause?**

Yes it does. There are many models that can be engaged with. Some of the models are given here,

a) The Non-Profit funds entirely the Brand creation however it uses a low cost approach by leveraging Public Relations and Events coupled with Digital marketing. There are many global social Events which are held every year where participation is free for non-profits and the Event organizers mobilize visitors. 'Social consumerism' is the theme of such events.

b) The non-profit can create a social communication model where the non-profit raises a small fund from donors for creating a Brand for beneficiaries, the beneficiaries pay 5% of the cost, the advertisement agency does free creative and media planning as a part of its 'social contribution' and a media house releases the communication for free as a part of its social action.

c) **The Government can fund the collective Brand creation, corporates can give in some money from their 'social responsibility corpus', the non-profit provides some funds from its own and some part of the fund comes from the beneficiaries**

128) **Can Non-Profits use collective brands to bring benefit to the communities they serve?**

Yes they can, they are already doing it and should do it more in future. In India 'Amul' is a collective Brand under which milk and milk products are sold. The sales are more than USD 3 bn and 90% of profit is distributed to poor farmers who supply milk. Similarly a non-profit co-operative society has created a Brand 'Lijjat Papad' (Papad is an Indian food product) and hundreds of poor women are working for this co-operative (non-profit ofcourse) getting livelihood. Many non-profits have created brands collective brands to sell 'coffee', 'Cocoa' and 'African forest products' to help their beneficiaries. Governments often help non-profit organizations to create collective brands and help 'clusters' of small producers who individually can't create a Brand for themselves.

129) How is the Brand Management deployed by non-profits in practice different from the way it is classically deployed by the companies?

The purpose of Brand creation for non-profits is generally not to create profits for themselves but to help their beneficiaries. It is thus a beneficiary driven activity not an investor driven activity. Secondly non-profits are in general more ethical in their communication compared to companies. Thirdly the Brand budgets of non-profits are much smaller compared to the companies. Fourthly the products being sold under the non-profit brands are either agricultural products or craft products or simple low technology products and not technically complex products as are sold by companies. Lastly on the Brand Management maturity scale, the non-profits score very low, their Brand Management is essentially a primitive Brand Management or a creativity led Brand Management and has not graduated enough to involve research led Brand Management or strategic Brand Management.

CREATING GLOBAL BRANDS

130) What is a global brand?

One definition is,' It is a Brand that derives more than 50% of its revenue from outside of its home country'. There are many other ways of defining it also. The central point is that when you operate in multiple countries, it becomes challenging to manage the Brand in each country according to that country's customers, culture, state of development, Brand positioning and so on. Managing customer research, advertising agencies, media tracking and positioning across every country is an even more arduous task.

131) What are the general approaches followed for global Brand Management?

There are three basic approaches that are followed for global Brand Management process,

a) Standardization
b) Localization
c) Glocalisation

In the first approach the company manages a Brand such that the Brand is positioned in the same way across all countries and communication released in each country is as near to each other as possible in ideational and visual terms. Johnson and Johnson is one such brand. There is standardization of the product, retail experience, corporate identity, brand identity and communication.

Localization refers to the approach where the same Brand is seen as a premium Brand in one country and a value for money Brand in another country. Take for instance Toyota Innova. It is seen as a premium vehicle in India and is used as a Taxi in Dubai. The positioning of the same product is different across every country. There is a customization of the product, Brand positioning, retail experience and so on.

The third approach is of Glocalisation which is mix of the above two in which certain parts of the Brand are kept standard across the world and certain aspects are localized to suit local tastes. McDonalds is an example of it where the Corporate Identity, Brand Identity and retail experience are standardized the world over, however the menu differs from country to country and communication is also customized to each country.

132) What are the differences in the process of Brand Management between managing a national and a global brand?

There is a world of difference between the two. Some of the points on which differences stand out are;

a) Each country has its own laws with regard to what can or can't be shown in advertisements, compare USA and Saudi Arabia

b) Language and Culture being different, communication in different countries is very different, compare Sweden and China

c) The positioning of the Global Brand (unlike in case of the national Brand) may or not be the same across countries and that creates multiple challenges

d) Each country has its own celebrities, its own domestic competition and its own media vehicles and customer's media habits which provides addition challenges to the Global Brand

e) Customer research in each country has to be done and it brings out often very different needs to be addressed which is not so complex in case of a national Brand

f) Managing advertising agencies in so many countries is a nightmare and so companies go for a global advertising agency with offices in all countries but then there is a cost to hire such an agency

g) Ensuring visual and ideational coherence across campaigns running across the year in all the countries is an arduous task both creatively and from quality control standpoint for a Global Brand

h) The cost of creating and maintaining a Global Brand is many times over that for a national Brand.

133) How do you select an advertising agency, do research and track release on a global scale?

It is virtually impossible for a company to hire a different advertising agency and a research company for each country and then co-ordinate with all of them. The same is true for trying to track communication released on multiple media vehicles for each country. Companies hence hire global advertising agencies, global research agencies and global media tracking agencies. Companies thus deal with a single point source for global operations. Sometimes companies appoint two global advertising agencies or two research agencies, giving a few countries to each to ensure healthy competition.

134) Do global brands get automatic protection as 'well known marks' across the globe or do they have to move a trade mark application in every country they operate in?

The concept of 'Well known marks' has come to stay which means that if any global Brand like LG or IBM or Toyota forgets to file an application in any country even then no applicant of that country can start using a Brand like these well-known global brands. It is deemed that these global brands are known worldwide and so deserve a protection worldwide. Global Brands today hence get protection as 'well known marks' across the world even without making an application in each of the countries they operate in. On the safer side however most Global companies file an application in every country and in every product sector, wherever they wish for protection.

As a Brand marketer, I'm a big believer in 'branding the customer experience', not just selling the service
John Sculley, CEO Apple

PART IV

BRAND SUCCESSES
AND
BRAND FAILURES

I was inspired by how Red Bull isn't about the drink; it isn't about the product or the 'Can'. Red Bull is a platform to celebrate all that humans are capable of accomplishing. They built a lifestyle movement, a Brand that sold this product.

Nick Woodman

We are really living the American dream, to be a successful Brand in the States and in Europe and to steep ourselves in our heritage. But we do it with a sense of humor. We don't take ourselves too seriously in fashion.

Tommy Hilfiger

BRAND SUCCESSES

Transforming a Brand into a socially responsible leader doesn't happen overnight by simply writing new marketing and advertising strategies. It takes effort to identify a vision that your customers will find credible and aligned with their values

Simon Mainwaring

135) Can three examples of Brand successes be given in the area of Consumer products? How is Brand success related (here) to Business success?

In case of consumer products 'Brand' has a very significant proportionate contribution towards 'Business successes'. Examples of three Brands are given here to enlighten the point,

a) Maggi

b) Sony

c) iPhone

Maggi is an instance of a great Brand success where the Brand Management efforts have complimented the product quality and over the years Maggi has established itself as an everyday product even in countries like India where traditionally, noodles were never consumed. It has taken efforts of more than 2 decades but the results are rewarding. The Brand Campaigns of Maggi deserve as much credit as the taste of Maggi in this Business success.

Sony is yet another instance where Brand Management could successfully capitalize on the product quality and innovation. Sony has come to signify very high quality and long product life. Thanks to good Brand Management the product quality has found an adequate reward and margin(s). Sony products sell at higher margins compared to most competitors. Some of the Brand campaigns of Sony have become classics in the annals of advertising, especially the campaign 'color like no other'.

iPhone is an instance where the public relations led pre-launch campaign created a world-wide excitement and anticipation. On the day of the launch the company had to worry about enough stocks and not about enough customers. It is the ideal case where good marketing makes sales redundant. Technological innovation, product design, product features, product quality and great Branding made possible the legendary iPhone success for Apple.

136) Can three examples of Brand successes be given in the area of Industrial products? How is Brand success related (here) to Business success?

In case of Industrial products, traditionally product purchase decision doesn't give much significance to 'Brand' and hence the contribution of 'Brand success' to 'Business Success' used to be marginal. However recent use of 'Branding' by Industrial product companies has created a new landscape.

Three examples in the context are discussed here,

> a) **Intel**
> b) **General Electric**
> c) **SAP**

Intel is a great example of how an industrial product is being sold under a consumer Brand with regard to its Pentium and Celeron range of chips. The Brand success of Intel has helped it survive and maintain margins in an increasingly commoditized micro-processor market. **Brand success of Intel** has contributed immensely to the Business success of Intel.

General Electric is today among the most respected brands with respect to efficiency and quality thanks to its highly acclaimed 6 sigma attainments. Although not many customers directly use GE products most customers would know about GE. Brand Management at GE has contributed significantly in enhancing the company's standing in the market and margins. GE found it easy to enter into consumer financing business since consumers already had respect for the GE Brand. Brand success at GE has contributed to its Business success especially in terms of margins and in instituting its consumer business.

SAP is again an Industrial Brand and the product is used by companies with large data processing requirements. SAP has created a distinct image for itself and its Brand Management has contributed significantly to its market standing and profits. Lay citizens who are not going to ever buy SAP also know of it as a good Brand. Today the Brand success is contributing to its margins however tomorrow when SAP goes on cloud for the small and medium enterprises and lay customers (may be with new use and pay products) the Brand of SAP will contribute even more to its Business success.

BRAND FAILURES

137) Can three examples of Business failure (or business loss) be given in the area of Consumer products? How is Brand Management aspect related (here) to the Business failure?

Three examples of business failure (or business loss) to elaborate a discussion in the area of Consumer products can be,

a) Nokia
b) Phillips
c) New Coke

In the instance of Nokia the Brand Management and quality aspect was good. Where the business failed was in the area of pricing and product features. It is an instance where although Brand Management was good the business failed owing to non-Brand reasons.

Phillips is yet another case where Brand Management is good however the product quality, price and after sales service is a difficulty. The company has become more like a design department of a university rather than a commercial company serving customers. Three decades back Phillips was a major Brand

in the Indian market, today it is on the margins with an insignificant market share owing to difficulties with its product quality.

Coke has always been in competition in Pepsi. Based on research Coke once had launched itself with a new taste called 'New Coke'. The product was accepted by customers in a blind test but was rejected in the market. The failure of this Brand launch was not because of product charactersticks or price but was solely because of Brand reasons. Customers saw Coke as a 'constant of their life' loaded with memories and intimacy. Coke had become a cultural icon far beyond a normal Brand. Customers could not take any 'change' in Coke. The company had to take back the launch and reestablish the 'classic coke'. This was a case of business loss owing to purely a Brand reason.

138) Can three examples of Business failure (or business loss) be given in the area of Industrial products? How is Brand Management aspect related (here) to the Business failure?

In case of Industrial products since Brand is not a critical decision influencing factor it is unlikely that any Industrial products business will fail owing to solely a Brand Management failure. Brand Management aspect hence may or may not be related to the Business failure (or Business loss). Three good examples to enlighten the point are given here,

- Exxon
- Corus
- L&T Cement

Exxon is an instance where the business failed owing to lack of ethics. The Brand of Exxon was a strong Brand till scandals broke out and after that there was little that the Brand could do. It is an instance of a business failure owing to non-Brand reasons. The Brand Exxon still has the possibility of being re-launched, hopefully by another company.

Corus is an instance of a business failure owing to Chinese dumping of steel in UK and other Corus markets. The Brand was a strong industrial Brand. The business failure (or loss) is thus due to international trade situation rather than owing to the Brand. The Corus Brand is still a strong Brand in the minds of the customers and has quite some latent Brand equity. Hopefully Corus will be re-launched someday.

L&T cement was a strong cement Brand in India. However the business had to be sold off given the capital intensive nature of the business and the financial burden it was causing to the company. The Brand fetched L&T a good amount of money given the high equity of the Brand. The strategic decision to sell off the cement division resulted in the death of the L&T Cement Brand. The Brand died for no fault of it's and ironically in its death fetched the company a handsome valuation.

Too many companies want their brands to reflect some idealized, perfected image of themselves. As a consequence, their brands acquire no texture, no character and no public trust
Richard Branson, Virgin

PART V   CONTEMPORARY   ISSUES   IN BRAND MANAGEMENT

a) Employer Branding

b) **Co-Branding**

c) PR led Brand Management

d) **Brand Commoditization**

e) Cause led Brand Management

f) **Experiential Brand Management**

g) Brand Management in a digital era

h) **Empty Brands**

The future belongs to brands that do more than pay lip-service to real dialogue and recognize that their customers want them to believe in something
James Murdoch, Chairman, News Corporation

CONTEMPORARY ISSUES IN BRAND MANAGEMENT

The ethics on which brands are built need to be ingrained in the business if the Brand proposition is to be credible to consumers
Paul Gaskell, The Value Engineers

139) **What is meant by Employee Branding?**

Employee Branding is the deployment of Brand Management for the purpose of attracting and retaining talent in the organization.

140) **Does Employee Branding work?**

It has been a partial success. Companies that had a great culture but was unknown to others outside have reaped great benefits by leveraging Employee Branding while companies with not a very good culture and trying to sell a bad product with good advertising have failed to harvest much out of Employee Branding. The central point is the company culture, Employee Branding can only act as a multiplier.

141) What is meant by Co-Branding?

Co-branding refers to two or more brands sharing expenses and risk to release a joint campaign inorder to benefit both the Brands. Intel and Microsoft have extensively deployed Co-Branding. Co-Branding is mostly practiced by companies with complementing products. Co-Branding is often practiced along with co-sales where bundled product offers are made to the customer.

142) Why Co-branding is not used extensively by most companies?

Co-Branding can be safely practiced only if two companies are not competing against each other in any market.

Secondly the two companies should have complementing products. Thirdly both companies should have comparable reputations lest one Brand is hurt being seen with another very small or less reputed Brand. Fourthly Co-Branding can be done if there is an agreement on who gains how much and who pays how much. Given these conditions are not easy to meet, Co-Branding is not pervasively used.

143) What is meant by PR (Public Relations) led Brand Management?

Many companies especially those who are in B2B space often create brands through campaigns where the main tool for communication is Public Relations. It takes more time than the classical route of an advertisement heavy campaign but yet it works well for many companies. It is one of the routes for low cost Brand Management. The limitation is it is not easy to achieve the 2-d graphical effects or 3-d audio-visual effects through public relations communication and so it creates a difficult situation to infuse certain associations in the mind of the audience, related to the Brand.

144) What is meant by Brand Commoditization?

Today there are too many Brands in any given product segment. In terms of communication also we are living in an over communicated society. Competition has led to too many companies releasing too much communication for Brand Management resulting in a clutter of communication. Audience finds it harder by the day to recollect which advertisement was for which product, since they see too many advertisements every day. It is also increasingly difficult to achieve product differentiation given intense competitive action by every company. This has led to a situation where companies put up brands in the market but the brands are selling like commodities more on basis of price than anything else. Having a Brand has become a hygiene factor to be in the market but is no longer the health factor that can bring in margins.

This phenomenon of Brand being bought almost as commodities by customers in the midst of a Brand and communication clutter is called Brand commoditization. Should you innovate like Apple did with iPhone, you can break out of the clutter and commoditization and then you can charge margins for a differentiated product.

145) **How do you overcome the dangers of Brand Commoditization?**
Innovation in technology, design, Brand campaign and Brand experience are the

ways to achieve true Brand differentiation and overcome the difficulty of Brand Commoditization. Innovation is at the heart of the enterprise.

146) What is meant by Cause led Brand Management?

Some brands occasionally align with a non-profit cause and release communication to that effect mostly either advocating a cause or promising to share profits from the sale of the Brand for a social cause. This combining of a 'social cause' with the Brand campaign is referred to as 'Cause led Brand Management'. Most company Brands use it as a Brand rejuvenation tactic. Brands created by non-profits (most of them) use the 'social cause' in most of their Brand campaigns on a continual basis.

147) What is experiential Brand Management?

We develop our experience of the Brand through; a) engagement with Brand communication b) product experience c) word of mouth and d) retail experience related to the brand.

For most Brands the focus of Brand Management is on communication. In case of Experience led Brand Management the focus shifts to engaging all the senses of the customer (or potential customer). It involves to a great extent the retail experience which involves gratifying the visual, audio, olfactory and tactile senses. This multi-sensory experience approach is referred to as Experiential Brand Management. The emphasis here shifts from experience of communication to a multi-sensory experience. Experiential Brand Management is practiced more in areas of Café, Designer Boutiques, Theme Parks and Thematic Hotels.

148) How is Brand Management different in the digital era than before?

In the digital era, the customer (audience) has choice of media. He can see television or net or mobile and through any other mode indulge himself. The content available to him is far more than before. The tools to entertain and educate him are also far more numerous than before. The hold the traditional media had on the viewer is far less today. People are empowered to create content and share it globally practically for free. Needless to say people are spending much of their time on digital content and digital devices.

This change in context creates challenges for companies, advertising agencies and media houses in areas of; a) content

creation b) reaching the audience c) monitor the efficacy of the campaign.

One has to create content, that can be used on all digital devices and not only television or press. Secondly media planning has become extremely complex, reaching the customer having become more difficult. Lastly audience and campaign research has become more complex as it involves far more interfaces and content therein.

149) **What is the concept of an Empty brand?**

Generally a Brand is created to sell a product. Is it possibly to imagine that you create a Brand without any product with you and then sell this Brand to some producer? This is the concept of the empty brand. The idea is to create a Brand just as you create a product today and then sell this 'created brand' to a willing buyer whose product and the Brand in question fit together.

Acceptance of the concept of the empty Brand will lead to an entire sector of Brands available for sale. The business of Empty Brands can be happen in two ways a) Venture Capital supported companies can create such Brands b) Advertising agencies and media agencies can come together to create special purpose vehicles which get into the business of empty brands, with or without support from external financers. Should it happen, citizens with Ideas and companies with a portfolio of Empty Brands will find a right.

150) How to study further the area of Brand Management after this book?

After this book, please see videos suggested in the annexure. Once done with it, please pick up the text book by

Keller on Brand Management. After that read books by Jack Trout, David Aaker, Kepferer and other classics on Brand Management and advertising. The entire list of suggested books, videos and other resources is given in the annexure. Lastly once you are comfortable in the area go on to read journals and research papers.

The future of brands is, in many ways, the future of business. Well-managed brands are the most efficient and effective creators of sustainable wealth

Richard Cordiner,
Planning Director, Leo Burnett

ANNEXURE

- Good Resources on Brand Management
  - **Books**
  - Websites
  - **Videos**

GOOD RESOURCES ON
BRAND MANAGEMENT

BOOKS

1) Positioning: The battle for your mind by Jack Trout and Al Ries
2) **Brand Positioning by Subroto Sen Gupta**
3) Ogilvy on Advertising by David Ogilvy
4) **Strategic Brand Management by Keller**
5) Managing Brand Equity by David Aaker
6) **Strategic Brand Management by Kepferer**
7) Building Brand Identity by Lynn Upshaw
8) **Retail Power Plays – Andrew Wileman**
9) Brand Failures by Matt Haig
10) **No Logo by Naomi Klein**

WEB SITES

1) https://en.wikipedia.org/wiki/Brand_Management
2) www.afaqs.com
3) www.interbrand.com
4) http://www.ogilvy.com/
5) www.millwardbrown.com
6) http://www.gecodesigns.com/
7) http://www.Managementstudyguide.com/brand-Management.htm
8) http://www.springer.com/business+%26+Management/journal/41262
9) http://www.capterra.com/brand-Management-software/
10) https://www.prophet.com/blog/aakeronbrands
11) http://www.sony.co.in/section/tvcommercial
12) http://www.coloribus.com/adsarchive/commercials/india/

VIDEOS

1) 1) https://www.youtube.com/watch?v=SBA_D19SWc0

2) https://www.youtube.com/watch?v=xVAi81SKRKA

3) https://www.youtube.com/watch?v=Knm-kuI_Pmk

4) https://www.youtube.com/watch?v=FtW1x5ouI6g

5) https://www.youtube.com/watch?v=9_XWp5fnXKc

6) https://www.youtube.com/watch?v=JKIAOZZritk

7) https://www.youtube.com/watch?v=uEKikAflGqk

8) https://www.youtube.com/watch?v=1l2CUjkg0ug

9) https://www.youtube.com/watch?v=GpPESJRuX4k

10) https://www.youtube.com/watch?v=A8CJPgD4t6Q

11) https://www.youtube.com/watch?v=Dxzg5SvUUaQ

12) **https://www.youtube.com/watch?v=fwyHM0bhflY**

13) https://www.youtube.com/watch?v=i-zMF9ouwno

14) **https://www.youtube.com/watch?v=wbFhyfXPalo**

15) https://www.youtube.com/watch?v=tK2ozWQ0HA4

about the author

Himanshu Vaidya is Management Consultant,
Trainer, Teacher and a Psychotherapist. He has
written on topics including Management,
Philosophy, Psychoanalysis and Spirituality.

He offers courses and training programmes in
areas of Psychoanalysis, Dream Analysis, Brand
Management, Corporate Social Responsibility
and Non-Profit Management.

He anchors a not for profit 'Brick Foundation'
with a focus on education and mental health.

write to the author at, hvindia@gmail.com

www.ingramcontent.com/pod-product-compliance
Lightning Source LLC
Chambersburg PA
CBHW081309170526
45166CB00011B/3457